MIRACLE LIVES OF CHINA

MIRACLE LIVES OF CHINA

BY
JONATHAN and ROSALIND GOFORTH,
(*Missionaries to China since 1888*)

Authors of
"How I Know God Answers Prayer"
"By My Spirit" etc.

SCRIPTURE TESTIMONY EDITION

WALKING TOGETHER PRESS
ESTES PARK · JENTA MANGORO

About the cover: This image is a studio portrait of Mr. Su and Mr. Goforth (seated). Mr. Su was one of the miracle lives recounted in this book. His story from alcoholic to evangelist to one of Mr. Goforth's personal assistants begins on page 113.

This image is in the public domain.

City of Toronto Archives, Fonds 553, Item 10.

Colorized by Jacoba Looije

© 2024 Walking Together Press

Published in 2024 by
Walking Together Press
Estes Park, Colorado USA
Jenta Mangoro, Jos, Plateau Nigeria
https://walkingtogether.life

ISBN: 978-1-961568-33-4

Cover design by D. Thaine Norris

Typeset in Adobe Garamond Pro by Peter Kurdor

1

ABOUT THE SCRIPTURE TESTIMONY EDITION

I T WAS the Apostle Paul who declared in his letter to the Romans, *"For I am not ashamed of the Good News of Christ, because it is the power of God for salvation for everyone who believes..."* (Romans 1:16). This truth must have resonated deeply with Paul, a former persecutor of the Church, who personally experienced the gospel's radical power to transform.

Miracle Lives of China paints a vivid portrait of this transformative power by telling the amazing and captivating stories of individuals—from addicted gamblers and learned scholars, to children, soldiers, and the aged—whose lives were radically altered by the redeeming power of the Gospel. This precious collection is a testament to God's enduring love. It reminds us that, regardless of our background or the depth of our sin, no life is beyond the reach of His saving grace.

Data science reveals trends and patterns in information. The *Scripture Testimony Index* is an extensive research project using artificial intelligence and data science to develop a New-Testament-driven subject index across a large body of missionary biographies and personal narratives. As the story enthusiasts at Walking Together Press study these books programmatically; beautiful, bright threads emerge—threads of prayer, provision, deliverance, specific leading, healing, transformation, revival, and miraculous conversion. The end result is an index of thousands of short story excerpts organized by subject and Bible verse that empirically demonstrate the truth of the Scriptures, and which is freely available on our website at walkingtogether.life. Another result of this research was the discovery of dozens of great books that are long out of print and in danger of being forgotten. The *Scripture Testimony Collection* is a set of such books that we enthusiastically recommend, to the degree that we are making the effort to republish them.

Walking Together Press has enhanced this classic title, *Miracle Lives of China,* by identifying and marking twenty-seven portions of the narrative that illustrate specific Biblical topics and verses. An extensive *Scripture Testimony Index* has also been added containing short summaries of how each Scriptural topic is illustrated, making locating specific stories easy. Furthermore, this title is one of many in the *Scripture Testimony Collection.*

To
Our Esteemed Mission Secretary
THE REV. ANDREW S. GRANT, DD.
This book is
Dedicated

PREFACE

For years we have felt a strong desire to put down in some permanent form the record of God's miraculous power in the conversion of men as we have seen it in our mission work in China. From time to time friends have urged us to write along these lines, but the strain of ever present service has been such, we have found it impossible to get down to the task. Within the past few weeks, however, a combination of circumstances have made the accomplishment of this work possible.

With the exception of Chapters II, V, VI and XIII, which are written by Mrs. Goforth, all the sketches were taken down from Dr. Goforth while he was lying blindfolded after a serious eye operation. In this connection we wish to express our deep appreciation of the timely and efficient help given us by Miss Margaret Gay, a former coworker in China.

We would also gratefully acknowledge the help and cooperation and inspiration received from many of our coworkers in the Honan Mission, throughout the years represented in these stories, some of whom are still carrying on. Some have passed to higher service. Then, too, the writing of these brief pen pictures has called to mind many others of our Chinese brethren and sisters of whom a record was not possible, and we can truly say that there are many, yes, very many other miracle lives that have not been touched on but which remain with us as precious memories.

Jonathan and Rosalind Goforth

Toronto, February 27, 1931

CONTENTS

About the Scripture Testimony Edition v

Preface ix

I. EARLIEST TROPHIES OF GRACE 1
1. The Blind Chief
2. The Humbling of a Proud Confucian Scholar
3. A Broken but Filled Vessel

II. TWO OF CHINA'S MERIT-SEEKERS 21
1. Nathanael
2. Nathanael's Friend

III. THE IDOL-MAKER 33

IV. THE MISSIONARY'S FARMER FRIEND 41

V. FROM SERVANT TO SUPERINTENDENT 47
1. The Yang Family
2. Yang Yu-ming, the Servant
3. Climbing the Ladder

VI. CAMEOS OF ONE CHINESE VILLAGE 57
1. Winning a Would-Be Murderer
2. How "Old Autocrat" Was Won by a Sketch

3. Little Mary and the Smallpox Babies

4. The Gambler's End

5. The Old Violinist

VII. THREE NOTABLE EVANGELISTS 73

1. A Military Mandarin

2. A Model Confucianist

3. A Scholar Saved from the Depths

VIII. PROOFS OF GOD'S GRACE 81

1. A Chinese Shakespeare

2. A Faithful Pastor

3. Saved from a Feed-basket

IX. HOW WE REACHED THE STUDENTS 93

X. NOTHING TOO HARD FOR OUR GOD 103

Among the Bandits

XI. THE STORY OF MR SU, MY TRUSTED CO-WORKER 113

XII. GOSPEL TRIUMPHS AMONG SCHOLARS
OF ONE COUNTY 119

The Story of Li Fu-poa

XIII. THE ANGEL OF SHANGHAI 129

XIV. THE BETHEL MISSION, SHANGHAI 137

A Work of Faith

XV. MARSHAL FENG YU-HSIANG 145

An Unfinished Sketch

Scripture Testimony Index 163

I. EARLIEST TROPHIES OF GRACE

Through all the depths of sin and loss,

Drops the plummet of the Cross;

Never yet abyss was found

Deeper than the Cross could sounds

—Anon.

I. THE BLIND CHIEF
(Chou Lao-chang)[1]

CHOU LAO-CHANG was Chief of Police for Hsunhsien. Any man to hold that position must possess great courage, great executive ability, and be without pity. He commands no stated salary, but he must raise it somehow. Besides, in order to do his work he must have dozens of underlings. These are his tentacles, reaching out to all parts of the county.

A murder case, especially if it be connected with well-to-do people, is a real bonanzza. He and his underlings will do everything possible to keep it from coming to the ears of the magistrate. Those who are guilty will be willing to pay anything in order to get the thing hushed up. I was told that

---

1 Pronounced Joe Lao-chang.

one year in a neighboring county there were a hundred murder cases that never came to the ears of the magistrate. The old chief and his underlings would get liberal "squeezes" in every case. Even in those cases that do come before the magistrate there is unlimited opportunity for "squeeze."

There is another very effective means for raising money. They will select some wealthy man who can be imposed upon. During the night the underlings will put a corpse over on his property. In the morning early they will come to his gate and say, "We have found a corpse on your land here."

The farmer, alarmed, will reply, "Why, I know nothing about it."

"That is all very well," the underlings reply, "but you must come with us to prison until you can prove that you did not kill him."

The poor victim will probably lose every foot of land before he can get out of their toils.

One of our well-to-do Christians once had this trick played upon him, but was able to get a message sent to me. I was on intimate terms with the magistrate of the county, and sent him a letter explaining that this man was a Christian and that it was impossible that he would be guilty of murder. The magistrate believed me and had him instantly released. There are endless devices that these devilish men are capable of inventing in order just to gain money.

Chou Lao-chang in many ways was a mightier man than the magistrate who ruled over the county. He was a native of the county and knew all about it. The magistrate would always be an outsider and had to pay a considerable sum in order to buy the position from higher officials. He could be fooled as to the real condition of things, but the chief of police never. The Chinese have a proverb in which they say, "You can hoodwink those above you, but not the ones below."

SCRIPTURE TESTIMONY
Disciples must keep their word
MATTHEW 5:37

Mr. Chou, the chief of police, found his sight going when he was around fifty years of age. In a few years he was totally blind, and for this reason had to yield his position to another. It was in the year 1889; Dr. McClure and I were visiting Hsunhsien. The magistrate received us very kindly, and had us take dinner with him. During our conversation the magistrate said: "My old chief of police is blind, and, Doctor, I would like you to have a look at him."

The doctor answered: "By all means, invite him in."

The chief came in, and when the doctor looked at his eyes he said: "It is cataract. I can readily cure that."

The chief of police was delighted beyond measure and exclaimed: "Doctor, go ahead right now and operate on them. I am ready."

The doctor replied: "But an operation like this would require at least two weeks for your eyes to heal under my supervision, and I have only two days to stay on this visit."

The look of disappointment that came over the old chief's face was pitiful to behold. He left us, but had not gone far before he let loose and reviled the doctor high and low. It is said he went on reviling the foreign doctor and his connections all the way home. He said: "The fraud! He knows he cannot cure my eyes, but he pretends before the magistrate that he can in order to keep up his reputation. He puts me off by telling me that he will come back again in six months. He is only a liar and deceiver like the rest of us."

Six months later to the day, Dr. Smith and I arrived at Hsunhsien, prepared to stay two weeks. The old chief at once came. The cataracts were removed from his eyes. The doctor held his hand before his eyes, saying, "How many fingers do you count?" The old chief, greatly delighted, cried out, "I see five." Immediately the bandages were put on, and the old chief was kept with us.

During those days we told him how much God loved him. At first it seemed incredible to him that God could love a man so wicked as he had been. Again and again we reiterated the fact that God's love is seen in the proof He gave when He sent His only Son to die for us; that Jesus Christ, God's Son, bore his sins on the Cross and all he had to do was to believe, and God for His Son's sake would pardon every sin. In a few days light had dawned and the old man was rejoicing that he was pardoned and saved.

It was God's wondrous providence to give us our first convert at Hsunhsien, which was the great idolatrous center for North Honan. This was the city of the far-famed

SCRIPTURE TESTIMONY
God leads believers in opposition to idolatry
ACTS 17:16-17 · I CORINTHIANS 8:4 · I JOHN 5:21

goddess who, it was said, could give male children. No Chinese would venture to die, if he could help it, without leaving a male heir to sacrifice at his grave and at the temple, and to send on supplies into the spirit world. Without such supplies he would be a beggar in the other life. He knows how hard a time beggars in this world have, and he does not care to suffer in that fashion for an eternity. Hence his one great hope is a son. A daughter cannot take the same place. She is early married off into another family and comes under the control of her mother-in-law. If the first wife does not bear a son, he will get a second wife. If the second wife does not bear him a son, he will get a third wife if he can afford it. But very few can afford it, because wives are expensive in China, as in other lands.

Now this famed goddess comes to meet the need. To any worshiper in need of a son she will give a flesh-and-blood baby boy in exchange for the offering of a paper baby at her shrine!

The writer remembers the time that he, along with Chou Lao-chang and others, was preaching on a hillside as the worshipers were crowding up to the goddess' temple. There was an unusually large crowd from the neighboring town, headed by the mayor, who had no son and was leading the procession with a paper baby in his hand.

The whole procession passed, but he stepped aside, for Chou Lao-chang was speaking in his vigorous manner, saying: "Yonder goddess has not any power to give you sons. I once thought she could. I once believed that all things were possible to her. When I realized my sight was going, I came and made her all manner of rich offerings. I even went to the expense of having special theatrical performances for her delight, hoping that she would pity me and restore my sight. The sight left my eyes and I became totally blind, and I had to feel my way about with a staff. Then the True God sent his servant, Dr. Smith, and he removed the cataracts from my eyes, and now I can see as well as ever again. Not only that, but the eyes of my dark heart have been opened. You know that I was chief of police for this county. You know that no good man can ever be chief of police. I was the most wicked and cruel man in the county. But the God of Heaven loved me and sent His Son to save me. I rest in His power and know that yonder goddess has not any power to harm me. I know that people are led astray through her priests, but I am not afraid. If she has any power, let her strike me dumb. She is nothing but a piece of clay. Why do you go up and bow down before her and make offerings to her when she has not any power?"

The mayor stood there with his mouth open, wondering. When Mr. Chou finished speaking, I followed. Among other things I said:

"I am one of ten brothers. My father and mother had ten sons and one daughter. My wife's father and mother had nine sons and four daughters. Here I represent two families where there were nineteen sons, and we never heard that there was such a being as a goddess who could give sons. From God's Word here that I hold in my hand we know there is only one Living and True God. He has all power in heaven and on earth. Life and death are completely under his control. If it be His will that you have a son or many sons, you will have them. If it be His will that you have no son, then you will have no son."

The other people were urging the mayor to go on with them up to make their offerings before the goddess. He threw his paper baby away, and said, "You may go. I am going to stay here and listen to this." After several hours he declared his stand for Jesus Christ and said that hereafter he would follow Him to the death. Within a year the mayor had led about forty families in his town to cast away their idols and turn to the Living God. Then a priest of Rome swooped down upon them and with all sorts of bribes led away thirty-six or thirty-seven families. We, in order to avoid making "rice Christians" need to go carefully, but Rome was only greedy for numbers. She could not, however, turn the mayor aside, for he had memorized the four Gospels.

Next year the mayor came to the fair. He joined with us in testifying and declaring the Gospel of the Grace of God. He was a very fluent and forceful speaker. Repeatedly he would declare to the crowds: "A year ago I came up here seeking a son from the goddess. On the way up to her temple I heard this Gospel of the Kingdom of God. I believed it and I threw my paper baby away, and now I want to tell you that the Lord has given me a splendid baby boy." The mayor afterward became one of our effective evangelists, and he with several other families maintained their faith in spite of all the enticements of Rome.

Mrs. Chou was as forceful a character as her husband. Before conversion, when aroused, her tongue was a terror to her opponents. She, too, became a humble follower of our Lord and Saviour. The two became earnest evangelists and preached the Gospel for many years.

It was at this great idolatrous center that we first saw the mighty movements of the Holy Spirit. One day while preaching on the portion of Scripture, "There is one Mediator between God and man, the man Christ Jesus," all in the room seemed to come under deep conviction. I heard a couple of the evangelists behind me exclaim, "Truly this is the same result that followed at Pentecost !" That same evening at another of the preaching-halls farther down the street we were preaching on the portion, "He bore our sins in His own body on the tree." The Spirit of God seemed to convict deeply the whole roomful. At the close, when I called for decisions, the whole audience instantly rose and declared that they wanted to follow this Jesus. I expected one of the evangelists to take my place and was turning around to turn the service over to him. I was astonished to see the whole nine or ten preachers standing there in amazement at what God had wrought. One took my place, and the rest of us all went into an inner room for prayer. We were in the room some minutes without anyone uttering a word. All seemed awed. Then one said, "Brethren, He for whom we have prayed so often, has been working among us tonight. Let us all be assured of this, that if we are to retain His presence we will need to walk carefully." Then each one led in earnest prayer.

SCRIPTURE TESTIMONY
God using an inner voice   *to communicate*
JOHN 14:26 · ACTS 10:19-20 · ACTS 11:12

Some days we would estimate that the crowd assembled at this religious festival would run up into hundreds of thousands. It was such an opportunity, that we as a mission each year concentrated on it. We would have from seventy-five to a hundred Chinese and Canadian workers carrying on preaching in many different parts of the grounds at the same time, and in rented halls, up till midnight each night.

One year the workers all gathered there, when there came such a heavy snowfall that the roads were all blocked and the people could not come to worship at the goddess' shrine. Seeing that the multitude was not a tithe of what it was usually, I proposed that we might spend several hours a day in hearing me give some addresses on the deepening of the spiritual life. This they readily consented to. One day after these devotional exercises were over, we were all to scatter to our different positions to preach. The committee in charge of arrangements that day said to me, "Your place this afternoon will be up on the hill top behind the goddess' temple." When the weather was good and the crowds were great, there was no better position than on the hill top. Now, however, few worshipers were in the city. The weather that day was bleak and cold. There was nothing to attract the people and they simply passed from one side of the hill to the other. That day I had been impressing with all the force I could muster that we should look to God for our audiences, that since God was more concerned about the salvation of men than we could be, we should look to Him in faith to bring us the people and hold them. But as I started out to go on to the hill top, the pressure from the Spirit of God was: "Practice what you preach. Illustrate in your own life what you have been impressing upon others." I could not help but reply, "Well, if I had been sent to the other side of the hill it might be all right, but not on the hill top." Still the pressure was the same. On arriving there I found the evangelist talking to two or three men. My coming aroused the natural curiosity of some passers-by, and soon there were fifteen or twenty people standing around us. The evangelist was one whom we regarded as a "great scatterer." When he started off afresh to preach to the larger number now gathered, they soon dwindled down again to two or three. All the time the pressure continued, "Illustrate in your own experience that which you have been impressing upon others." I replied, "Lord, if the evangelist had stopped when I came up and I had been able to start in then when the people were showing curiosity in the foreigner, I might have been able to get a crowd and hold them, but now the crowd is all scattered again." Still the pressure was the same, "Illustrate in your own experience what you have been impressing upon others." At last, when things were at the lowest ebb, the evangelist ceased preaching and turned it over to me. There were no people standing on the hill. There were just those who were going back and forth. It was cold and windy and the people were not inclined to stand around. I commenced with two or three, but when I became conscious of my surroundings I could not turn around, the crowd was pressing me so closely on every side. I talked through one address, and still the crowd was increasing. I talked through another address, and then through the third. By this time the sun had gone down over the Shansi hills in the west and we let the crowds scatter.

That night in every one of our preaching-halls men were going forward inquiring. They said they had become interested up on the hill top that afternoon.

Several days later a well-dressed young man came in to ask for all the different books we had, saying, "I was with my uncle on the hill top the other afternoon, and we were convinced that this was the doctrine of the True God. We bought several books then, but we want to buy every kind you have. The sins of my life have to go," he continued, "since this Saviour has come into it"; and holding up a fancy water pipe, he said, "This among other things has to go too."

From this center the Gospel of the Grace of God has gone out in all directions and groups of believers have been springing up far and near. Hsunhsien, being the very citadel of idolatry for North Honan, would be zealously guarded by the great adversary of souls. There were scores of priests resident in the temples at that center, and the city was noted for having many of its gentry zealous idolaters. Naturally a mighty opposition to Christianity might be expected to spring up.

On one occasion when our whole force were at work there, reports came to us that strong opposition was organized and that we might expect trouble. The old chief of police, Mr. Chou, went to his underlings, whose respect and support he still could call upon. He got them to go out to the heads of the opposition and give clear warning that no open attack would be tolerated. The following day some young priests, in passing where the chief and some of the rest of us were preaching, gave vent to some very uncomplimentary utterances. At once the old chief let loose. His voice was like the roar of a lion. An avalanche of words flowed from him. Although the language was not altogether Christian, it was very expressive, and the young priests slunk away like whipped curs. That evening the old chief sent word to their superiors that they should keep the young priests in order. That was the end of all opposition. How the good hand of our God was manifest at such an idolatrous center, to give us a chief of police for our first convert!

Mrs. Chou died at the age of seventy-six and her husband at seventy-eight, earnest and faithful witnesses to the end.

2.THE HUMBLING OF A PROUD CONFUCIAN SCHOLAR
(Wang Feng-ao)[1]

The acquisition of the Chinese language is a big task. It is conceded by all experts to be a very difficult language. But it is not impossible for anyone with ordinary linguistic gifts to acquire it, providing that along with such they have the perseverance of the saints.

SCRIPTURE TESTIMONY
Salvation transforms
2 CORINTHIANS 5:16-17 · GALATIANS 6:15

The writer was simply one of that kind. Coming to China under thirty years of age, he has been able to get a fair working knowledge of the language. It certainly is a glad day when a missionary can hold an audience as well as if in his native land. When you see a Chinese audience held as quiet and moved as deeply as would be possible in your homeland, then you may know that you are using this foreign language in an effective manner.

There is no royal road to gain the Chinese language. The only way is to sit down with a Chinese teacher and plod away. Most men will drop into the blues more than once before they attain it. Some women are apt to have a cry once or twice before they get there.

Mr. MacGillivray and myself invited a Mr. Wang Feng-ao to be our teacher. He was a man of high scholarship and recommended as a very able teacher. We had been in the country a considerable time by then, and required more advanced instruction. This Mr. Wang seemed to be everything that we could desire. Shortly after the agreement had been made a neighbor of his dropped in.

---

1 Pronounced Wong Fung-ow.

"I hear you have invited Mr. Wang to be your teacher," said he.

"Yes," I said. "Don't you think we are very fortunate in securing a man with his great gifts?"

"Yes," he replied, "perhaps. But Mr. Wang has a very bad temper. He never has been able to hold a position long, just because of that weakness, therefore I don't think you foreigners will bear long with him."

About that time Dr. McClure and Mr. MacGillivray went into Honan, and Mr. Wang and his wife accompanied them. For some months longer I remained at Lin Ch'ing. On moving into Honan it was arranged that Mr. Wang should help me in the forenoon, and Mr. MacGillivray in the afternoon. During the months he had been in Honan he had taken offense at something. He refused to attend a religious service, and would not allow his wife to, either.

The first morning he came to my study to commence work I said: "Mr. Wang, you put me in a rather awkward position. The Lord Jesus has commanded me to go and preach His Gospel to every creature. If I don't obey I offend Him. But I hear that you say that you won't listen to anyone declaring this Gospel. Therefore, if I declare this Gospel to you, I offend you. What am I to do?"

"Well," said he, "I guess if you view it in that light, there is nothing for it but for me to listen."

That morning we commenced the study of *The Evidences of Christianity*, by Dr. Martin. The first reference that the subject called up was Matthew 25:14, etc.

"Mr. Wang," I said, "you see from this parable that talents are given according to the ability of the one receiving them. From the one who has received great talents His Lord will expect the more. You know that in your country many may have ability, but their families are too poor to give them a chance for schooling. You were not so situated. You have attained unto great scholarship. You are capable of holding any position in the land. Supposing Jesus Christ called you away today to take account of the use you have made of these talents and opportunities, how would you stand?"

The question hit home and he humbly said: "Don't ask how it would fare with me if I came before the Lord Jesus Christ. Ask how it would fare with me if I came before our sage Confucius. I can quote from memory the teachings of my sage, but I don't practice them. He says, 'Do not unto others what you would not have others do unto you.' I have disobeyed and even reviled my parents. I have been drunk repeatedly and have said and done most unlawful things. I have gambled, smoked opium, and gone to harlot houses. If I passed before the sage today he would condemn me as an unworthy follower of his. If that be so of a man like Confucius, how could I ever stand before God?"

We never once urged him to come to any of our religious services, but day by day as we studied we looked up together the Scripture references.

After about six weeks had passed, Mr. Wang, to the surprise of everyone, came in to morning worship. He read his Scripture verse in turn, and when all rose to pray he stood with us. A little while after, when he came to study with me, I said:

"Mr. Wang, I was so overjoyed to see you in the meeting this morning." His eyes filled with tears as he replied: "I prayed last night for the first time in my life. In a vision or dream I walked outside the west gate of my native city. You know how it is situated. The west gate opens out on to the river. As you go out you have to turn southwest. The city wall is on one side, and the river bank on the other. Soon there is a deep depression, and when the summer rains come the road becomes a bog. In my dream I turned south and went right into the bog up to my chin. I became very much alarmed. I thought if I took another step I might be smothered in the bog. Just then Mr. MacGillivray and yourself, walking on the river bank, said in astonishment, 'Mr. Wang, what do you mean by going into such a dangerous place as that?' With that I awoke, and it came over me with a rush of conviction that the way I had taken was the way of sin and unbelief and the end would be destruction, whereas the way that you are urging me to take is the way of life eternal. Instantly I got out of bed, and on my knees I prayed that God would forgive me, a sinner, and I believe He has done so."

Mr. Wang then went on to say, "That very first morning when you spoke to me of the talents I was deeply convicted, and the conviction never left me."

Many rejoiced at the change that had come over Mr. Wang. The proud Confucian scholar was humbled before Jesus Christ. He at once commenced attending all services, and allowed his wife to come, too. Some time previously Mrs. Wang came timidly in one evening to see my wife, saying, "Mr. Wang has gone out, uptown, and it is safe for me to come to see you and inquire from you the way of salvation." She said: "If my husband were in the yard I would not dare come. He would beat me if he found out." She listened to the Gospel as long as she dared, and then hurried home. As soon as Mr. Wang had taken his stand for the Lord, she came forward rejoicing, for she had long been a secret believer.

When we invited Mr. Wang to become language-teacher I presented him with a fine copy of the Bible in the Mandarin language. At the time apparently he thanked me most heartily. It was merely lest he might give offense. He poured scorn and ridicule upon me behind my back.

"The idea of giving me, a scholar, a Mandarin Bible, with the language so simple that it speaks of 'we, you, they'". For months he cast it aside and would not look at it. A hint of this was conveyed to me, and I bought him one of the deepest Wenli (classical) Bibles. After his conversion I saw him constantly reading the Mandarin Bible. I remarked, "Mr. Wang, I gave you that Wenli Bible, but I never see you using it."

"No, since Jesus Christ has come into my heart, and the Holy Spirit has enlightened me, I realize how profound His book is. I am like a child; I know nothing at all. I just revel in this simple language into which the Bible has been translated.

Mr. Wang became active in testifying to the Grace of God, and whenever he had opportunity he accompanied us to the street or to the villages round about to tell of his new-found faith. When we opened the important prefectural city of Changte, Mr. Wang, then an evangelist, was the all-important man. Again and again before the city god temple in the heart of the city, when we had great crowds standing around us, Mr. Wang would then declare:

"I am now a true follower of the sage Confucius. Before the Almighty God changed my heart and gave a new and right spirit to me, I disgraced our great sage by my wrong living. I could talk well and on the highest ethical themes, as all we Confucian scholars do, but I was vile in heart and vile in word and vile in deed." Then he would tell how the devil had led him astray in the past, and how wrong had been his life, and how he had disgraced the name of the great Confucius.

"But now for many months" he continued, "I have lived in your city. What man among you has ever found me in the haunts of vice that you frequent? Who among you can recall word or deed of mine that did dishonor to our great sage? It is all because Jesus Christ, the Son of God, dwells in my heart by faith. I am now strengthened with might by His Spirit, so that the things I once loved I now hate, and the good deeds that I formerly knew I ought to do but did not do I now perform through God's saving power."

During these times of testimony every eye in the crowd would be riveted on him and conviction seemed to be written on the faces of all. Later on, when the prefectural city of Weihweifu was opened, on all hands it was thought that Mr. Wang was the man of first importance to be used there. A year or so later, when it was agreed that the prefectural city of Hwaiking should be opened, Mr. Wang was the man chosen; and when, the sainted Craigie Hood was dying with cholera in that city, Mr. Wang was the only Christian brother who ministered unto him.

At the outset when we invited Mr. Wang to become our language-teacher, we were warned that his temper was such that it would be impossible to keep him long with us. The Lord, however, took control of even his temper when He gave him a new heart and a right spirit. Once I saw Mr. Wang's Christianity put to the severest of tests. Provincial jealousies in China are notorious. Even Christians of one province will form cliques against Christians of another province. This provincial jealousy is such that sometimes it is impossible to get Christians from two adjoining provinces to work harmoniously together.

Mr. Wang was the only man at that time we had from an outside province. The Honan Christian leaders commenced to bring up such serious charges against him that we felt we could not go on any longer without an investigation. Mr. Wang was brought in to face his accusers. In the most quiet Christian spirit he listened to all these charges, and then brought such absolute proof of his innocence that even those who brought the charges saw that they were unfounded. We then thought that Mr. Wang would retaliate upon these men as they deserved, but he never said one disparaging word; he never seemed to hold the slightest resentment toward any of those who made the charges, but on the other hand seemed to love them more whole-heartedly than ever.

Mr. Wang to the end walked with God and labored earnestly for the salvation of others, then in triumph went to be with his Lord. We praise God for His grace abounding in the life and death of our language-teacher and second convert, Wang Feng-ao.

3. A BROKEN BUT FILLED VESSEL
(Wang Fu-lin)[1]

SCRIPTURE TESTIMONY
Jesus is able to save to the uttermost
HEBREWS 7:25

In China about fifty years ago, before they had newspapers, story-telling was very popular. It was about the only way the people gained outside information. A storyteller was supposed to tell about everything ancient and modern, at home or abroad. Wang Fu-lin as a storyteller was above the average. For hours each night he would hold large crowds, and thus made a good living.

When quite young he fell into the opium habit. This affected his throat so that as time passed he lost his clear silvery tones and was obliged to give up story-telling; then, to make a living, he ran a gambling tent, at fairs and theatricals.

When we first met this man he was thirty-eight years of age and a total physical and spiritual wreck. He was a bent-over, skin-and-bone skeleton. At that time I spent ten days in his home town. Each afternoon I saw Wang Fu-lin with his opium outfit going over to the west room of the inn to ease the craving. One evening he sat down before me in a crowded room. I turned to him, almost in tears, and said: "Wang Fu-lin, I tremble for you. The road you have chosen leads straight to hell. You tell us you

---

1   Pronounced Wong Foo-lin

cannot resist the craving here, but the craving yonder may be increased ten thousand fold, and there you will not be able to obtain even opium ashes to ease it."

The poor fellow answered with a broken voice: "I know what you say is only too true. I have read twice through the New Testament and am well aware of the fate which awaits me. I have tried so often to break loose from this awful grip of opium that I have now given up in despair. I must go on to the bitter end."

"Wang Fu-lin," I said, "you must not speak in that fashion. There is hope in our Saviour. He can save to the uttermost all who come unto God through Him. Go over to Chuwang and see what Dr. Malcolm can do for you."

"How could I walk such a distance?" he asked. "It is forty-five li away and to save my life I could not walk five li."

"But there is a way," I urged. "They are sending a cart for me, and you can come along." I had taken typhoid fever but did not know it. Word had been sent home to Chuwang of my daily increasing fever and a cart was being sent for me.

Wang Fu-lin continued to object: "There is no use in my going, for the doctor would not receive me as a patient without my paying down fifteen hundred cash, and I have not even five cash to my name."

This was only too true, for he had squandered away everything and did not possess a foot of land. The fifteen hundred cash demanded by the doctor was not because he coveted the money of a poor opium slave, but through this means he sought to stiffen the man's resolution. The opium addict had to pay down fifteen hundred cash, which he could ill afford. After a few days, when the craving seemed unbearable, he would feel like pulling out and returning home; but the thought of the money he had paid in, which he begrudged losing, helped him to stick it out to get the worth of his money. The doctor usually returned the money when the cure seemed complete.

Again I turned to Wang Fu-lin, unwilling to give him up, and said:

"Don't mind about the money; I will make that all right with Dr. Malcolm. Just come along with me." He came, and was received into the hospital.

The doctor warned me: "You will have to do your part. The medicine is little more than a blind. Try as much as possible to keep him from thinking about himself and his misery."

We had him brought to our house several times a day, giving him tea and cake and showing him pictures of the West and praying with him. On the fifth day he seemed like a man demented. I arranged for a man to be with him every moment to keep him from climbing over the wall and going up the street to get opium. After the fifth day the extreme suffering seemed to be eased. By the fifteenth day he left us, apparently delivered from all craving.

Before Wang Fu-lin returned to his home I asked him, "Would you mind telling me just how you felt on that fifth day when you appeared to be in such agony and acted so strangely.

He replied: "My misery that day was awful. On the fifth night I thought I was awake, but perhaps it was a dream. It came over me so strongly how hopeless it was to fight against the craving any longer. I started for the south end of the house, intending to climb over the wall there. When I reached the place I was amazed to find a deep and wide pit between me and the wall. I felt I could not jump that far and if I failed I would certainly break my neck by falling into the pit. Just then a fiendish-looking creature on the inside of the wall and on the farther side of the pit beckoned to me, saying: 'Jump over. You can easily make it. Just jump. Don't play the fool any longer. You can get rid of this opium craving. Jump across, go up the street and get the opium.'"

"Several times I went to the edge of the pit, intending to spring across. Then I heard a Voice above and behind me urging, 'Wang Fu-lin, resist, resist.' The realization of my appalling danger came over me. It seemed that this was God's last warning. If I gave way He might forsake me forever. I there and then resolved that, if I died, I would die resisting. Almost instantly the craving eased off, and I fell asleep."

An opium-user is the last man to suddenly place in a position of trust. We knew the family were in dire straits, and we needed assistance badly in the work of proclaiming the Gospel, but we left Wang Fu-lin alone for almost two years, not daring to use him without clear guidance. During those years he and the whole family were tested to the utmost, at times being brought to the verge of starvation, sometimes having only leaves of the trees to eat.

In October of 1895 I took my wife and children to Changte. A foreign woman and children had never been seen in that region before. When the

SCRIPTURE TESTIMONY
God's work will not lack God's supply
PHILIPPIANS 4:19

news spread abroad that these strange beings had arrived in the north suburb of Changte, the people, young and old, men and women, by thousands flocked there. It was a common thing for us to have our windows banked with faces curiously watching us take our breakfast, and from then on till sundown we would not be free from crowds. The question ever present with us was, How could we make the most of this wonderful opportunity to win the people's friendship and to make known to them the Gospel? The men were received and preached to in the front court, while the women and children went back to the inner court, where my wife and children were.

I had at that time not even one evangelist to help me, neither had my wife a Bible woman. Besides the strain of reaching these crowds, I had the oversight of building and the hundred and one calls incident to the planting of a new mission station. Sometimes when feeling unable to stand the strain of preaching longer I would receive a note from my wife, begging me to come to her assistance and relieve her by speaking to the women, as her voice had given out. Two weeks of this brought us both to a place of desperation. One day I went to my wife and, pointing to the words, "My God shall supply all your need according to his riches in Christ Jesus," I asked, "Do we really believe this? If we do, let us kneel down and ask the Lord to send us some one to help us in preaching the Gospel." Later my wife said that while I was praying it seemed like asking for rain from a clear sky to expect such help when we had not even one convert in the Changte district. But God answered and that without delay, for the following day Wang Fu-lin started from his home to come to us.

But how unlike he was to our idea of a God-given helper on his reaching our mission gateway. His appearance was exactly that of a professional beggar—toes visible through shoes and socks, his hat torn, and a patched-up gown so stiff with grease that it looked as though it could stand alone. Truly "the Lord seeth not as man seeth." But, oh, how glad I was to see him!

At once I said: "Wang Fu-lin, I believe God has sent you to help us at this time, Will you stay and preach for us? I cannot give you wages (this was against the rules, since he had not been appointed by the mission), but I can give you your meals."

"Of course I'll stay," he replied. "I can get nothing to do at home and my staying here will be one less mouth to fill there."

It was out of the question that Wang Fu-lin, as he appeared on his arrival, could be put on the platform to face audiences in which were often gentry, official secretaries, and others of the educated class. In those days I wore Chinese clothes; it was, therefore, an easy thing to have the man clothed out in one of my second-rate suits. He looked well as I left him preaching in the chapel.

All the old story-telling powers seemed to come back to him, and the Chinese later had a saying that, if Wang Fu-lin wanted to get an idea into your head, you could not escape till he had succeeded in getting it there. One outstanding characteristic of his preaching was that in logical order he would bring one fact after another in cumulative effect until all opposition was broken down and you were forced to accept his conclusions.

A Chinese story-teller takes great liberties with his facts, and Wang Fu-lin was no exception, The Bible stories glowed in living fashion while he held up the characters before his audience. This was especially true of the prodigal son. He knew the story well, for he himself had dwelt in the far country and had fed on husks with swine. He told the story with telling power, assuring his hearers at the close that since God had saved him, the chief of sinners, there was hope for everyone.

Wang Fu-lin could talk with power for an almost endless time. On one occasion when I was compelled to go into the city I asked a visiting evangelist to take my place in the chapel. On my return and after eating my dinner, I went to the chapel. Here I found Wang Fu-lin preaching as vigorously as ever. As he was leaving I said:

"Of course Mr. Li relieved you by taking my place."

"No," he replied, "no one has been here."

Later I found Mr. Li had forgotten and had gone into the city on his own account and Wang Fu-lin had continued preaching for upwards of three hours.

From the beginning of his ministry with us, converts sprang up everywhere, both in the city and throughout the country. During those days our chapel was always full and Wang Fu-lin never tired of telling the story of redeeming grace and exalting his Lord and Saviour.

For three years the Lord spared him to preach with ever increasing spiritual power, though with ever increasing physical weakness. Wang knew his time was short and always spoke as "a dying man to dying men." At first other members of the mission were unwilling that we should take him in even as gatekeeper, but when his marvelous preaching power became evident to all, they urged me to spare no expense, but to feed him on the best food possible to keep up his strength, and this we did.

During the few years he was spared to witness to the abounding grace of God, Wang Fu-lin was the means of winning all his relations to Christ. For many years now there has been a self-supporting Christian Church in Hsintsun, his home town, which was always known as notoriously bad; yet it was from such a place God raised up his servant to give proof of the wondrous power of His great salvation.

Since in those early days at Changte we had no medical work, it was a case of pure evangelism, preaching the Gospel, and many will forever praise God that they heard that Gospel of God's Grace through Wang Fu-lin. The foundation then was laid so wide and deep that one of the most noted Chinese evangelists, who recently held special meetings throughout the Changte region, stated he had never met in all his ministry throughout China a work of Christianity equal to that seen in the Changte region.

Wang Fu-lin, the redeemed story-teller, went on proclaiming the story of the Cross until his strength failed and he triumphantly passed into the presence of his Redeemer and King. Though more than thirty years have passed since his death, he is still spoken of as "The Spirit- filled preacher."

II. TWO OF CHINA'S MERIT-SEEKERS

I. NATHANAEL

"Behold an Israelite indeed in whom is no guile"
(Wang-Mei)[1]

MANY OF China's so-called religious sects are closely allied to Buddhism. The "Merit-seekers" (Hsing- shan-ti) are almost entirely recruited from these sects. Their ethical standards raise

SCRIPTURE TESTIMONY
By faith, those who believe in Jesus are truly saved
JOHN 10:1-14 · ACTS 13:38-39 · ROMANS 10:13 · COLOSSIANS 2:13-14 · I JOHN 4:17

them morally somewhat above the average heathen, and not infrequently sincere seekers after something higher and better are found among them.

This was true of Wang-Mei, a young man who, with his family and many of his neighbors, belonged to one of the more aggressive of these religious bodies known as the *Sheng Tao*, or Holy Road. Wang-Mei went much further than his family and friends in seeking to accumulate merit for the future life. Many long pilgrimages were taken by him on foot to great religious centers of heathen worship, till most of the renowned shrines were visited. One of these journeys took him five hundred English miles south of his home; another as great a distance to the north, and

---

1 Pronounced Wong-May.

still another many hundreds of miles westward. Thus he became known throughout a wide region as a "holy man."

The belief that the greater the suffering of a pilgrim the greater the merit placed to his credit led Wang-Mei and other pilgrims to adopt various means to this end, such as wearing heavy wadded garments in hot and thin garments in cold weather when ascending the pilgrims' path up to the mountain-top shrines. (Most, if not all, the great temples are on hill or mountain tops.)

But all this failed to give Wang-Mei the heart satisfaction and peace he craved for, and he determined to forsake his wife and children and enter a hermit's retreat far off to the west of his home. How long he remained there I do not know, but, in February, 1894, Wang-Mei left his hermit's home to visit the shrine of the famous goddess at Hsunhsien during the winter festival held in her honor. Knowing as we do the wickedness surrounding and permeating to the very core the worship of this goddess, and knowing also the gentle nature and deep heart yearnings of the young man at this time, we do not doubt but that he came down the mountain with his heart doubly longing for something different.

And surely we cannot but believe that a Divine Presence guided his feet that day as he passed down the street, for as he came to the Christian preaching-hall he stopped and stepped inside, simply curious to see what was going on. The Rev. Mr. MacGillivray was preaching on the text, "By grace are ye saved through faith: and that not of yourselves; it is the gift of God. Not of works lest any man should boast" (Eph. 2 :8, 9.). Could anything have been more timely? But as Wang-Mei listened he became more and more annoyed. He put question after question to the speaker. Finally he demanded, angrily:

"Do you mean to say that all my years of merit-making go for nothing?"

Absolutely nothing," replied the missionary.

This was too much for the merit-maker, and he left the meeting in hot indignation. But God's guiding hand had not been withdrawn. Wang-Mei had a friend, Ho-I, an idol-maker. This friend, who had become somewhat interested in the foreigners' teaching, tried to persuade Wang-Mei to go with him to see the missionaries at Chu Wang. Although Wang-Mei had fully determined to drop all thought of a new way of grace, he finally consented to accompany his friend to the mission. They arrived at sundown when the missionaries were taking their needed exercise by a brisk game of tennis. This filled Wang-Mei with disgust, for he could not conceive how men representing God could act in such a manner; (That he later completely changed his mind on this point we shall see.) The following morning early they returned home without even

asking to see a missionary, and Wang-Mei again resolved to look no further into the matter. But his friend Ho-I, who had by this time become a secret believer, persuaded him to read some Christian books of his. The Lord used these books to convince Wang-Mei of the truth of salvation *by grace alone.*

The revealing of this truth and the reception of Christ as his living, loving Saviour brought great joy and peace into his soul. He could well have said with another of God's children:

> "Long did I toil and knew no earthly rest;
>   Far did I rove and found no certain home;
> At last I found them on my Saviour's breast.
> With him I found a home, a rest Divine,
> And I since then am His and He is mine."

He had found such peace as he had never dreamed could be his, and with this new-found joy and peace came a longing to tell others about it all.

From this time on the two friends, so different from each other, zealously propagated the Christian faith, and it was indeed remarkable how many of our converts at that time came from the religious sect to which Wang-Mei had belonged. The following will throw some light on how this came to be. One of Wang-Mei's first acts after he became a Christian was to write a letter to a friend living fifty *li* to the west among the foothills. This friend, named Chang, belonged with his family to the same sect as had Wang-Mei. The letter told how he, Wang-Mei, had found that which they were seeking and urged them to go to the mission at Changte. In his letter he quoted a common Chinese saying, "All—literally *ten thousand*— sects must bend at last to one." Some time later a missionary touring in the region found this family ready and waiting for the Gospel. So the truth became propagated through the early believers.

A year passed, and so many had become Christians through the testimony of Wang-Mei and Ho-I, that the missionaries from the newly opened mission station of Changte were invited to visit their homes to examine candidates for probation. The missionaries found most of the adult members of both these families ready for recording, and the prospects for the founding of a Christian church in this region were very bright. But scarcely had the missionaries reached home when the Roman Catholics, hearing of the movement, sent in their agents, and with tempting promises of free schools and a soup kitchen they bought up the young weak converts in the faith, and practically all went over to them.

But young though Wang-Mei was in the faith, his belief was too well founded on *grace to* be easily turned aside. A few days with the Roman Catholics were sufficient to convince him of his error and he returned to us. A little later his wife, father, and stepmother, also Ho-I and his family, returned, but the rest remained with the Romanists, thus causing in that region a permanent breach in the company of Christian seekers.

For a time Wang-Mei's knowledge of truth and Christian experience were gained under fire. He accompanied the missionary on his evangelistic tours, and even in those early days did much good by his splendid testimony to what the grace of God in Christ had done for him. During this period he made remarkable progress in the knowledge of God's Book. When our first boys' school was opened and a good trustworthy teacher was needed to take charge, Wang-Mei was appointed to the position. Then it was that he became an enthusiastic tennis-player. Among other ways of healthy exercise the boys were taught tennis and Wang-Mei thoroughly enjoyed his games with them. But before he had been in charge of the school two years his marked evangelistic gifts and knowledge of the Bible led the missionaries to appoint him to the work of evangelism, while one of his pupils took his place in the school.

Of the years which followed, of his faithful successful service, and of the blessed influence of his life upon those most closely associated with him, others who worked with him could write better than I; and lest I be thought to overdraw in what I am about to write, it is well to state that the facts now given are practically word for word as my husband stated them to me.

During the fourteen years of Wang-Mei's service in the mission the missionaries *could find no fault with him!*

Patient, kind, sympathetic, gentle, yet zealous for the truth, he became honored and loved by all. But his two outstanding characteristics were *gentleness* and *sincerity*. We missionaries came to always speak of him as "our Nathanael." On one occasion, when the furlough of one of our co-workers, the Rev. John Griffith, was due, he came to my husband saying, "I could go to Canada with an easy mind if you would let me have Wang-Mei to put in charge of my work. But it seems scarcely fair that I ask for your *very best man.*" Dr. Goforth gladly agreed to Mr. Griffith's request, saying, "Do not worry about me, for the Lord always gives me as good if not a better man when I part with one."

We give but one illustration of the high regard in which Wang-Mei was held by all the missionaries. If there was an out-station becoming cold and back-slidden, Wang-Mei was the one chosen to revive it. Was there a difficult important mission for which a trusted Chinese was needed, Wang-Mei was the one to whom the missionaries most naturally turned. During the Boxer year, when the faith and courage of all were tested to the utmost, Wang-Mei faced danger and persecution unflinchingly, and by his example and exhortation he helped to strengthen his weaker brethren and steady the faith of many who would probably have failed during that period of overwhelming darkness and danger.

Close beside the mission compound at Changte a number of small cottages had been erected for the accommodation of mission workers and their families. For some time Wang Mei's wife and two boys had made their home in one of these cottages.

One day the sad news was passed around that Wang-Mei had been carried in from a country out-station on a stretcher and was lying in his home at the point of death from pneumonia. Though earnest prayer ascended for his life which we thought was so needed in the great harvest field around us, God saw best to take him. Shortly after reaching his home our beloved Nathanael sank into unconsciousness, and the following morning passed into the presence of his Master by whose grace alone he was saved.

We must now tell the story of Chang Ming-san, one of the many brought to Christ through Wang-Mei. We group these two together not only because of their warm friendship, but because they both stand out, in the absence of sordidness and depravity in their lives previous to becoming Christians, in marked contrast to most of our Christians.

2. NATHANAEL'S FRIEND

"True gold fears not the fire"

—*Chinese Proverb*
(Chang Ming-san)

One evening in the early autumn of 1894 a solitary fanner could have been seen on the summit of a many-terraced hill among the foothills west of Changte. The man rested wearily on his hoe, for he had worked, with a brief respite for morning and noon meals, since dawn of day. Had his little farm, of one and a half English acres, been in one field, how simple and easy would have been the task of working it. But, alas! it was not. Instead the land, which had come down to him from his father, was divided into *seventy* distinct terraces or plots, reaching up a steep hillside, the earth being kept in place by stone supports, the keeping of these in repair consuming not a small share of the farmer's time and strength. To get the best returns from the two yearly crops he might hope to reap if rain did not fail, he must needs labor during every hour of daylight for nine months of the year. Only so could he hope to do his part in providing for his mother, wife, and three children, for Chang Ming- san was the only son of his mother, and she was a widow.

As the sun dipped in a blaze of glory behind the long dark-blue line of the beautiful Shansi Mountains, the farmer watched with reverent interest until the last rays had disappeared, then bent his head in worship, for the sun was one of his many gods. Slowly turning, he wended his way down the hillside to the little village nestling in the sheltered valley below.

The village, and indeed the entire region, contained no family more respected and well spoken of than the one I am about to introduce to my readers. The story is not an imaginary one, but is the simple record of those we once knew and loved.

The Chang family were poor, *grindingly* poor farmers. They belonged to the uncountable class who lived their life span on "the ragged edge of ruin." It was necessary for each member of the family to do his or her part in supplementing the general income. The old mother, when not on long pilgrimages, spun thread and wove cloth. The young wife fussed and fretted and fumed and worked through each day as it came. Even the children had at an early age to learn to do their part: the eldest, a boy of ten, had his daily quota of fuel to scrape up of dead roots or grass by the roadside. But the heaviest task of all fell to the second boy, who, although only six years of age, was the nurse of his younger brother, a strong, healthy boy of nearly two. This child, when clothed in the heavy padded winter garments, was indeed a formidable bundle for even an adult to hold; how a child of six could manage such a burden must needs be seen to be understood.

Mr. Chang was at this time in the prime of life, under thirty, tall, well proportioned, with a remarkably intelligent, *good* face, such as we seldom met with in the land so stamped with sensuality. From his earliest childhood Chang Ming-san had accompanied his mother on her many yearly pilgrimages to sacred shrines and temples, for she was a devoted member of the Buddhist sect called the Holy Road. When still a mere lad Mr. Chang joined the sect, and while not as ostentatious in his religion as his mother, seemed more sincere in seeking after something better, higher, truer, than what he had. Indeed, it was doubtless these heart-yearnings after *peace* and *purity* which gave such expression to his countenance and color to his life that he became known far beyond his native village as "the *truly* good man."

Not far distant from Mr. Chang's home lived a Buddhist hermit in a cave retreat. As the winter drew near and the days shortened, farm work slackened, and often Mr. Chang took the path leading to the hermit's cave, carrying with him, from his own meager store, gifts of eggs or vegetables. One day on reaching the retreat he found a visitor had arrived who proved to be no other than the renowned Wang-Mei (our Nathanael).

From their first meeting Wang-Mei and Mr. Chang drew together as only kindred souls could do. In the weeks that followed while Wang-Mei remained with the hermit, Mr. Chang had often to face stormy tongues from wife and mother because of his long absences from home. At such times he was with his new-found friend, often watching and worshiping the setting sun together. We can only imagine something of what passed between these two during those times, for each was hungering alike for the same peace and rest of soul.

When at last the time came for Wang-Mei to leave, their parting words were very suggestive:

"Friend Chang" said Wang-Mei, "if you ever learn the secret of peace for which we are both seeking, will you promise to let me know?"

"Wang-Mei, my brother," replied Mr. Chang, "I will indeed. And if you first get this peace, promise you will share it with me."

Wang-Mei promised, and so they parted.

Not many months later a flutter of excitement passed over the little village where the Changs lived, for had not a letter come for Chang Mingsan? This letter was from Wang-Mei. He told his friend how he had found that for which they were seeking, and that he would come in person to tell him all about the wonderful truth he had discovered.

The letter was shortly followed by Wang-Mei himself, bringing with him a missionary, the Rev. Donald Mac-Gillivray. This missionary, on his return to Changte, told how he had found a family away among the foothills just ripe for the old, old story, and of the joy he had in telling into eager, ready hearts the message of salvation. Though many years have passed since then, there comes the clear remembrance of what this little incident was to us all. They were the dark, uphill days when we were fighting against great odds—against heathenish hatred and superstition. To hear of hearts *eager* for the Gospel was indeed a bright glint of hope in the great darkness around us.

Both Mr. Chang and his mother accepted Christ before the missionary left. The household gods were at once taken down and destroyed, while the heathen villagers looked on from a distance to see what dire calamities would come upon those who dared to treat the gods so. Strange it is that in this case, as in the case of many another pioneer Christian, what followed gave the heathen all too good ground to believe they were right.

Just at this time I became desperate for some one to help me in receiving and preaching to the crowds of women who daily thronged our home. God heard my cry for help. A letter was sent off to old Mrs. Chang, asking her to come and help me. She responded to the call, and proved herself to be a truly God-given helper in time of need. The fact that she had for years been a "woman preacher" in the Buddhist sect gave her training along certain lines which proved of great value to her when proclaiming the Gospel of Jesus Christ.

For a long time Mr. Chang remained the only Christian throughout a wide section of the hill country. His faithful and fearless testimony led not a few to become at least *secret* believers. From the first his wife gave him untold sorrow through her bitter opposition to what she and the neighbors called "following the foreign devils." Then the series of testings began which added fear to her fury.

The second son, a bright, healthy little fellow, became suddenly ill, and in a few hours had passed away. In vain did the poor distracted mother call upon her neighbors to join in calling for the child's spirit to return. In vain the father sought to comfort her, but she refused to be comforted and blamed the father for angering the gods. In the sad weeks following the death of the boy the father had only the comfort of his new-found faith to sustain him in the petty persecutions showered upon him wherever he turned.

Then again death entered the home and claimed the youngest boy, the baby. On hearing the sad news we sent old Mrs. Chang home to try and comfort the heart-broken mother. But a sadder blow awaited her. At the first sight of her beloved son her mother instinct told her some dread disease had fastened its hold upon him. She lost no time in having him taken by cart to the mission hospital at Changte. The doctor's verdict was very definite— "Rapid consumption; no hope."

Though over thirty-five years have passed since the day Mr. Chang entered our home for the first and last time, I can see the scene as if it were yesterday; Mr. Goforth supporting him on one side and the old mother on the other, Mr. Chang was led to and laid upon our sofa. Here he lay for some time. The stamp of Christ-likeness on his countenance was wonderful. He was all joy and hope. As he left our home after that brief visit there remained the consciousness that one had been very near the borderland.

But a few weeks passed after reaching home when the end drew near. Neighbors who had been unkind and bitter in their persecution now began to show him their old love and respect. The mother went to stay with him to the last, and even the wife became subdued and sought to serve him the best she could. Not long before the end he asked his wife to stay beside him. Taking her hand, he said, "Wife, won't you take Jesus as your Saviour?" She hesitated. Again he pleaded with her to accept the Saviour. Overcome, she burst into tears and was on the point of yielding, when a heathen uncle standing near whispered in her ear: "Don't yield for worlds. See how the gods kill all who oppose them." Hearing this, the poor woman became so terrified she rushed out into the court and refused to return.

The dying man, calling his mother, asked that his hands and face might be washed, and when this was done said, "I want to be all ready when my Saviour comes." A little later a look of wonderful peace and joy came into his eyes, and in a brief moment he was gone.

During the winter of 1921, following the great famine, we with a band of evangelists visited the main out-stations of Changte. On this occasion we had a wonderful reception on arriving at the town of Hopei, near Chang Ming-san's old home. A body of soldiers came out to meet us, and we were escorted through the streets with banners flying, drums beating, and a great tooting of horns. We were taken to the largest and finest temple, where every arrangement had been made for our comfort during our stay there. A well-organized and self-supporting church made us recall the early beginnings of Christianity. It was on this visit that Mr. Chang's widow, for many years a Christian, related to me many of the facts recorded here.

"What about the old mother?" some have asked. For years old Mrs. Chang worked faithfully through those hard pioneer years as our first Bible woman. In 1900, when the fearful Boxer persecution arose, the faithful old Christian stood firm even to possible death. She was hung up to a tree by her thumbs and would have died so, but under cover of darkness friendly neighbors, possibly secret believers, came and released her. On our return to Changte after the uprising was over, she was one of the first to greet us, and for three years longer worked for her Master until called Home.

III. THE IDOL-MAKER

Saved from the depths, to Serve
(Ho-I)[1]

Ho-I was by trade an idol-maker and temple-painter. He gained great proficiency in his calling. Many of the gods in several counties were of his handiwork. As a painter of temple scenes no one could excel him. Having a wild, wayward disposition, he naturally became acquainted and associated with most of the rough characters of several counties. This opened up endless ways to break laws and indulge in evil practices. Many times each year he would be seized and taken before the magistrate and beaten. He became, when still in his early years, completely beyond the control of his parents.

Ho-I was in fact a natural-born fighter, for he seemed to be in his element when a fight was on. Throughout his entire home region he was always the chosen leader in village wars so common in China. At thirty years of age he was as deep down in the pit of iniquity as the evil one could drag him. His reputation was notorious. He had an elder brother who was, if anything, even worse than himself, but this man, Ho-Liang, heard Mr. Mac- Gillivary and others proclaiming the Gospel, and decided to become a Christian. This infuriated Ho-I to such a degree he determined to waylay Mr. MacGillivary, murder him, and throw him into one of the

---

1   Pronounced Hé-ee.

irrigation wells which dot the countryside. In this he failed, for he could never find Mr. MacGillivary free from one or more Chinese companions.

About this time he went with Wang-Mei on a pilgrimage to the shrine of the goddess, mention of whom is frequently made in these sketches. There he intently listened to the proclamation of the Gospel by many different speakers. Being almost convinced that we were preaching the truth of the Living God, he bought books with the intention of searching into this matter more deeply.

Strange to say, his decision for Christ was made before Wang-Mei took his stand as a Christian. The two were warm friends and neighbors, though as far apart as the poles in character and life. Yet it was the notoriously bad Ho-I—just a "sinner saved by grace"—who led the well-known "holy man," Wang-Mei, to accept salvation through the finished work of another.

It was not long before the missionaries at Changte received an invitation from Ho-I and Wang-Mei to visit their village, as practically all the members of both families were eager to become Christians and were ready for the necessary examination which was required before they could become probationers. The missionaries were delighted with what they saw was the result of the two first Christians faithful witness among their own people. But, alas! scarcely had the missionaries reached their homes when word came of trouble having arisen through the Romanists.

The priests of Rome, hearing of the movement, sent their agents to lead these people away from us. They told them that they were being fooled by joining up with the Protestants, that these Protestants, being misled by a monster of a man named Luther, four hundred years ago, were cast off by the Roman Catholic Church, that the Protestants had no power or prestige at all, and that in times of persecution they would be at the mercy of their enemies.

"You are safe," they said, "in joining this great Roman Catholic Church because we have the great Kingdom of France to back us. Besides, these Protestants do not really love you like we do; they will not manage your lawsuits nor teach your children free. You have to pay for everything you get from them. But think of the wonderful love of our great head, the Pope of Rome. At this very time he is sending boatloads of treasure over to China to be used in helping all who will join us."

Can we blame these young converts? They knew that Rome had great power in the law-courts. They also knew that all who went to the Roman Catholic Church, and sent their children there, were looked after free of charge. Ho-I and Wang-Mei went to the Romanist mission. Ho-I even took his children along and started them in their school. Wang-Mei, as soon as he saw the image of the Virgin Mary, began to question and make it awkward for the Romanist leaders. When they said, "This is just the image of the Blessed Virgin." Wang-Mei replied, "But what is the difference between the image of the Blessed Virgin and the image of the Goddess of Mercy? In either case, is it not equally an idol?" To pacify Wang-Mei they removed the image to another room.

In a few days these two friends came back to us, both convinced that the worship of Rome was full of idolatry, the same as that which they had left. Both men were now fully settled in the faith of Jesus Christ. The difficulty, however, with Mr. Ho was how to get his children out of the Romanist school. We talked the matter over, and I said, plainly, "There is nothing for it but for you to lose all face and go in and bring them home. He started off, and next day came back with the children. He just wept for joy over the great deliverance. From that time onward there was not a shadow of a doubt with these two men but that they had found the true way.

I commenced to take them around with me everywhere, and taught them how to preach under fire. In those early days we had much opposition to meet with. Soon it became quite clear that Mr, Ho was in his element when opposition arose. It required opposition to bring out the best in him. He could on occasion roar out like a lion, and again be as gentle as a lamb. His past life experience in evil ways gave him a thorough knowledge of men, even the worst.

We both gained experience, as time went on, in dealing with rough crowds. We were once driven pellmell off a fair ground because we did not take the precaution to get our backs up against a wall. We realized our mistake when it was too late. Chinese as a rule, even the worst, will not offend within the range of your eye, but they take liberties behind your back. That day we were soon made a football of, for in turning to remonstrate with those at our back,, those in front were just as bad. There was nothing for it but to retire ignominiously from the field under showers of clods. Ever after we took the precaution to get our backs against a wall. Then as long as the wall stood we could stand as much pressure as the rest of them. Sometimes clods would fly, but the clods were as apt to hit the other fellow as us, and then they were angry, and it soon ceased. At these times I had the utmost confidence in Mr. Ho that he would beat down opposition. While I generally let him take the lead, I would be praying that God might use him just to meet our opponents with that resourceful wit in reply that he so fully possessed. We never failed to finally overcome and get a hearing with the worst crowds when our backs were against the wall. It was a capital way to get up the language, and the experiences of these hard-fought fields were invaluable. Never once did I get into a tight situation but the resourceful Ho-I would find a way out. Rather than submit to exorbitant demands, he himself would wheel our barrow or carry our baggage.

SCRIPTURE TESTIMONY
Beaten for preaching the Gospel
ACTS 5:40 · ACTS 14:19-20

Then 1900, the Boxer year, came upon us. Rumors of dreadful happenings were constantly reaching us. When the country work became really dangerous, Mr. Ho and I concentrated on Changte city. We worked a great deal among the thousands of soldiers who were then assembling in the Changte region, and succeeded in making fast friends of many of them. Day by day we would take our place in the center of the city before the prefect's *yamen*. Repeatedly have I heard Mr. Ho say, when he gave the story of his past wicked life:

"I constantly broke the laws of our land; I was constantly being brought into disgrace by my misdeeds. Many times in this very court now before us I have been publicly condemned and beaten. But years have passed since I believed in the Lord Jesus Christ, the Son of God, He saved me to the uttermost, so that I don't want to sin as I once did. Since the Lord took control of my life, never once have I been disgraced in this court-house."

At last conditions became so disturbed even in the city, the friendly officials asked as a favor that we would cease public preaching on the streets lest a riot might ensue.

About that time a message came from our consul-general advising us to flee to the coast as quickly as possible. It seemed unfair to our Chinese converts that in time of danger we should pull out and leave them. After consultation among ourselves, we missionaries all decided to stay and take the consequences. When we informed Mr. Ho and the other Chinese leaders, they went away quietly, saying nothing. Next day they returned, saying: "You have decided to stay and take the consequences. Since that is your decision, we Chinese believers will stand with you, even if death be the result. But as we see it, you should obey your government's order through your consul. Go now, and we will scatter among our Chinese friends, for we will be the same as the rest of them and will likely escape destruction. If you stay here, we all are apt to be massacred together and the cause of Christ will perish. If you leave now, you may return to us again when this storm blows over."

Getting this decision from the Chinese, we had no further hesitation as to the line of duty.

As soon as preparations could be made and all missionaries assembled we started south towards Hankow. Knowing Mr. Ho's fearlessness, we begged him not to court danger by remaining in our compound. We urged that their lives were the important thing; the foreign property did not matter. After we went away Mr. Ho failed to take our advice. He remained on in charge of the compound. The officials came out and seized him and had him beaten and dragged into the city. He said the crowds densely packed the streets right into the official court-house. Laughs and jeers greeted him on every side. "The foreign devils have fled, and their dupes, 'devils number two' are in a fix. Defile him, kill him, quarter him!" were common epithets. He said the only ones that gave him the slightest word of sympathy that day were soldiers whom we had led to see the right way.

Preliminary to the trial, an official left him in an outer room of the court-house with the window opening onto the great court, which was packed with an expectant crowd. Seeing this good opportunity for preaching the Gospel, Mr. Ho could not let it slip, so from that vantageground he proclaimed Jesus Christ and Him crucified. The astonished crowd remarked: "Surely these Chinese have eaten the foreign-devil medicine.

They have gone crazy. They are totally devoid of shame. Think of this fellow, after passing through all this disgrace that he has gone through so far, still talking this Jesus doctrine." Then he was brought before the magistrate. While he knelt there his Honor asked:

"How comes it that you have become a follower of these foreign devils? What can you Chinese hope to gain by it? You disgrace yourselves and your country."

Mr. Ho replied: "Your Honor, I am not following the foreigners. I am following the Living and True God. This Living and True God loved us and sent His Son to die in our room and stead, so that He might save us from our sins and their consequences. The gods that I have hitherto worshiped, and that you all worship, are not gods at all. I am by profession an idol-maker. These hands of mine have made many of the gods worshiped now throughout our county. If the people of any place wanted a little god, these hands of mine made the little god for them. If they wanted a big god they gave me more money, and I made a big god for them. But now I clearly see that it was impossible that my feeble hands could make a god which could be anything but a curse to those who worship it. I once was so bad that I broke all our laws. I wouldn't obey my own parents. I wouldn't obey my 'father and mother official.' Consequently, many times each year I was condemned and beaten in this very court of justice. But ever since God took possession of my life, never once have I been condemned or beaten."

The astonished official did not know what to reply. He hesitated, and then said: "Go home. I'll protect you."

Mr. Ho went home. We had left money in the bank sufficient to pay the salaries of all the Chinese workers, but the banker concluded that when we foreigners had fled there would be no further demands on that money, therefore he refused to pay out a cent to any of our workers, though we had arranged for him to do so. He readily paid up, however, when we foreigners returned. Mr. Ho and his family and Wang-Mei and his family were in desperate straits. Practically famine was on. Owing to the lack of spring rains, no planting was done. July had arrived, with little hope of any possible harvest. But Mr. Ho was always a man of resource and a difficult situation was bound to bring out his latent powers. He opened a food shop, and he and his family cooked food and carried it to all the surrounding country for sale. He made enough not only to keep his own family, but also Wang-Mei's, from starving.

Famine fever in times of destitution is inevitable. Finally Mr. Ho, his wife and five children, were all down at the same time with it. They were so helpless that not one of them could even rise and get a cup of cold water for another. Just then, when they had come to extremity, their heathen relations and neighbors in the form of Job's comforters came in to remind them that the gods had got even with them at last.

"You see, you have offended the gods beyond measure, and you have yourselves alone to blame for this affliction that has overtaken you. But even yet, if you will sincerely repent, the gods may be merciful and pardon you. Let us go and buy new gods and put them up on your walls, and burn incense for you since you can't get up to do it. The gods may then be pleased to spare you." It was a cruel test. Even Mrs. Ho commenced to plead with her husband to give way.

"We are all about to die, and there is no hope for us. Let us yield and go back to our forsaken gods," said she.

Mr. Ho in reply ordered all to leave his house at once, saying: "We are done forever with idolatry and false gods. If we perish at this time, we perish, trusting in the only Living and True God."

All departed, believing them hopelessly misled by the "foreign devils." That evening Mr. Ho was able to get up and wait on the others, and after a few days all were well again.

As soon as Mr. Ho was sufficiently recovered he felt he must go to the west, where the Christians were under sore persecution. He knew that region like a book, and all the roughs in it. His former evil friends turned against him. They stripped him to his waist, and suspended him from a tree limb by cords tied to his thumbs. Then as he hung there in agony, they beat him with rods. Soon, however, they let him down, not daring to go too far, since the magistrate at Changte had let him off without punishment.

Upon our return after the Boxer storm had passed, I went around with Mr. Ho to comfort all the Christians who had weathered the storm, and naturally there was great rejoicing. In closing I wish to state that in all our association together, for over thirty years, never one cross word passed between Mr. Ho and myself. He was the most faithful of friends. I could trust him to go anywhere and carry out a commission for the good of the cause. Though now seventy years of age, he is still carrying on. How we praise God for giving us such a capable co-worker, taking him right from the depths of iniquity and transforming him into an open channel of His Grace. Surely with such a transformed life before us we could never doubt the power and grace and goodness of God. To save one such man out of China's hundreds of millions would be abundantly worth while. The tragic pity of it all is that comparatively so few in Western lands have caught the vision.

IV. THE MISSIONARY'S FARMER FRIEND
(Wang-I)[1]

WANG-I, OF Ta Kwan-Chwang, was the most influential man in his town of more than fifteen hundred people, and he was probably the wealthiest. He with many others were zealous religionists in the same sect to which Wang-Mei belonged. Wang-I was led into the light by Ho-I and Wang-Mei. At first it was his plan to remain Nicodemus-like and await the coming out of the whole village before announcing himself a Christian. In fact, he went so far as to write a letter requesting me not to visit his village till he had one hundred who believed as he did; then he would come to me. But his fellow villagers were slower in coming out than he had expected. Then things were hastened for him by the remarkable conversion of the very worst character in the town.

Up to that time, though I had sent repeated invitations for him to visit us, he did not come. Then one day he was announced, and I hastened out to meet him. We had tea in our study and a good chat before my wife played the organ, and ran up seams on the sewing-machine for him to take home and show the womenfolk. We took him through all the rooms and into the kitchen, where he was very interested in the kitchen stove.

When we supposed he might have seen enough to satisfy his curiosity he asked if he might not see the cellar. On going to the cellar he lifted the lid of every box and jar and peered in.

---

1 Pronounced Wong-ee.

"Well! if our people are not the worst liars in creation! Men from my own town have declared to us that they had been down in your cellar and with their own eyes saw many jars of children's flesh salted down!"

A few days later Wang-I returned with seven of the chief men of his town to see us. Over a cup of tea we talked to them of God's love in the gift of His Son. Wang-I then led them to hear the organ and see the wonderful performance of the sewing-machine! He had them see all the strong points of the kitchen stove, and then led them down into the cellar, where he planned a triumph!

After he was sure that they had carefully looked into every box and jar he asked, "Where is the children's flesh we have heard so much about?" Some of them looked very sheepish, as if they had been caught, and all agreed it was nonsense to believe such stories. Wang-I then took them all into the city and gave them a good dinner.

Within a week Wang-I was back again, and this time with a big four-wheeled wagon drawn by six mules and loaded down with women. He walked in in triumph with his aunt and his wife and about fifteen other leading women of his town. They gazed in wonder at the strange foreign children, and, so clean, too, and at the children's mother with her natural-sized feet. Then Wang-I, holding up a big foot, said to the women, "See! this foreign woman can stand steady and move around with ease, for her feet are as large as mine!" We sang "Jesus loves me" at the organ and we thought they would never tire of the performances of the sewing-machine. After examining the beds in the different rooms they came to the kitchen, where they expressed much wonder about the cooking-stove. By this time they were all so happy over their reception and what they had seen that they showed no hesitation or fear over following Wang-I down cellar. He made them look carefully into everything and ridiculed the absurd stories which had been circulated.

Now these mothers had confidence that there was no danger of losing their little ones if they accepted this Jesus religion.

It was a happy lot of women who packed into the big wagon for the return journey. Naturally they became eager witnesses of what they had seen and heard and the work at Ta Kwan-Chwang grew apace for the Lord.

Twenty-six out of twenty-eight members of Wang-I's own family turned to the Lord. No one need be surprised at the size of Wang-I's family, for, like every other Chinese family, it was made up of uncles and aunts, nephews and nieces, sons and daughters, daughters-in-law and grandchildren. As long as they lived in one compound and cooked their food in one big kettle, they were reckoned one family. By the time the Boxer storm burst upon us in 1900, Christianity had found entrance into nineteen families in Ta Kvvan-Chwang. Throughout the years a very close friendship existed between Wang-I and ourselves.

We fled from Changte June 28, 1900, and I returned early in January, 1902. The following day I hastened out to Ta Kwan-Chwang. There in

SCRIPTURE TESTIMONY
Holy Spirit convicts people of their sin
JOHN 16:8

Wang I's home we all met and rejoiced greatly, for the Lord had brought us through. None had been killed, though many of us had found out what it was to carry around on our bodies the marks of the Lord Jesus. Our hearts were full of hope that since our God had kept us He was going to do great things through us.

But the cause at Ta Kwan-Chwang did not continue to prosper. I was no longer in control there, for it had been deemed wise that we get work started in the many large centers in the northern part of the Changte field. Wang-I continued to visit our home as usual, and on such occasions we would ask about the outlook around his center. Every time his answer was: "Not very good. You know that we of ourselves can do nothing. When God's time comes He will certainly save." According to Wang-I, God had decided for the time being to let the people of his center perish, notwithstanding that He had given His Son to die for them and had sent the Holy Spirit to see that that amazing sacrifice should be made effective. We knew that Wang-I was wrong and that most likely the hold-up was in himself, but there was no visible sin we could point to.

Thus did the cause of God at Ta Kvvan-Chwang fail to prosper until November, 1908. At that time there was perfect unanimity among Chinese and foreign leaders alike that we must have God's revival through the outpouring of the Holy Spirit. Being convinced that since Wang-I was the chief man in the Ta Kwan-Chwang church, the hindrance must be with him, therefore I made a special effort to have him at all the meetings. Imagine our disappointment when we saw his son appear instead of himself.

"Why didn't your father come?" I asked.

"Well, he says he is old and will soon pass on, and that I ought to learn all I can, so as to take his place."

"Very well," I said. "Stay a couple of days and see."

After two days the son was mightily broken, so we told him that he must go home to let his father come. "Tell your father," we said, "that we can accept no excuse. If he does not come he will offend his best friend."

Next morning Wang-I arrived, apparently not overpleased. "You should not have sent my son home to get me. I am old and of no use and will soon leave this world. He is young and should have stayed to learn, and moreover I haven't any sins to get rid of."

I replied, "Tarry a day or two."

Two mornings later Mr. Ho came in to me and said: Wang-I is in a terrible state of agitation on account of his sin. Last night around midnight we were all talking over the situation which is upon us when Wang-I fell to the floor as if shot, crying out, 'My sins! Oh, my sins!" He has been weeping ever since and no one can comfort him. At his request I have come to ask if you will not start the meeting in the tent as soon as you finish breakfast. He wants to get a chance to confess his sins!"

After breakfast I hurried out to commence the meeting. On arriving at the second court, Wang-I came to meet me with tears flowing down his big cheeks. Unable to speak, he grasped my arm. We both went weeping into the tent. He knelt on the platform, crying loudly, while hundreds of people filed in. When he could command his voice he cried out:

"It is my sin which has hindered God at Ta Kwan-Chwang. I always made excuse, saying God's time hasn't come. It wasn't God's time which hadn't come, but Wang-I's. When I came before the magistrate to get indemnity for what the Boxers had robbed me of in 1900, I lied. The Boxers robbed me of three mules; I swore it was six. Of a hundred and fifty bushels of wheat; I swore it was three hundred. Of two hundred bushels of millet; I swore four hundred. I have become rich through my lying and have grieved the Holy Spirit. I will make restitution and will build a church for Ta Kwa Chwang." Wang-I kept his promise and built the church. On our last visit, when my wife and I went there with the evangelistic band, the church was too small for the crowds which came, and a large mat tent was put up. They listened with remarkable patience for hours at a time, and when the main meetings were dismissed we went to the inquiry-room to find it full of men and boys seeking salvation.

Wang-I when almost eighty, high in the esteem of thousands of Christians, passed into the presence of the King of kings. What a privilege to have a share in the salvation of such splendid men!

V. FROM SERVANT TO SUPERINTENDENT

I. THE YANG FAMILY

"They that honour Me I will honour"

ALMOST HALF the village of Yuantsun, situated two miles from our mission gate, belonged to an old family named Yang. All the compounds north of the one village street were occupied by various branches of this one family. The Yang relationships were a constant puzzle to the missionary from the west. For instance, one member of the Yang clan would introduce another thus:

"Pastor, this is my younger brother."

The missionary, as a result of long experience in ways Chinese, would then ask:

"Is he your *own* brother?"

"Well, not quite. He is the younger son of my great-nephew." Then perhaps turning to another standing by, would say: "This is a more distant relation (literally "*a turn-the-corner brother*") for my cousin's brother-in-law is married to his eldest brother's wife's sister!"

The Yang's courts seemed almost as complex as their relationships, for each compound had a perfect string of them leading back to the open fields beyond. These courts always seemed congested with an indescribable conglomeration of rubbish piles, pigs, chickens, and swarms of children. I only wish I dared draw a picture of these children as I have seen them in

47

all seasons of the year. You, my reader, must try and read between the lines when I say that their clothes were made like thickly wadded bed-quilts, and were put on at the approach of cool weather and on they remained all winter and into the early summer, when they were discarded with great delight for the cooler nature's brown! But I will spare you, and to my story.

One afternoon in the late autumn of 1895 a well-to-do farmer was returning home after selling his vegetables in the city of Changte, and as he reached our mission gate he was attracted by the sound of a man talking inside. The natural instinct of a Chinese, whose strongest characteristic is curiosity, caused the man to stop. Wondering to himself if he dared venture within, for he had heard strange and bad stories about the foreigners who had just moved in there, he slowly pushed the great gate open wider and, looking well to right and left, he made his way across the court to the room from whence the sound came, and found himself inside a large room well filled with men. They were all so intent on listening to the preacher, no one seemed conscious of a new arrival. Seating himself just within the door, he spent some time in getting used to his surroundings; but suddenly his attention became so riveted on the speaker and on what he was saying, all else was forgotten.

Wang Fu-lin, that wonderful Spirit-filled evangelist, was the preacher. His appearance was certainly against him. The tall, emaciated form was stooped, but not with age, for he could not have seen fifty years; his skin was like a piece of parchment, with the dark livid hue of the inveterate opium-user, and every few sentences were interrupted by a cough which shook his whole frame. How could this man hold an audience of heathen men, for hours at a time, simply spellbound? How, but by the power of God which rested so manifestly upon him and enabled him to see almost daily men yield themselves to God, although at that time the persecution against Christians was so great it meant facing terrible odds to take an open stand for Christ.

This afternoon Wang Fu-lin was telling his favourite story—the prodigal son. We will not dwell upon the liberties he took with the Bible version in giving it a Chinese setting; it was enough for him that his hearers saw the picture of the father and his lost son as he had seen and been won by it. That he succeeded in this was evident, for not a man moved, and our friend, the farmer, quite unconsciously, moved up bench by bench until he was directly in front of the speaker. Towards the close of his address Wang Fu-lin told his own story and showed how he was the prodigal son and how his father had taken him back, cured him of his opium, cleansed him from his mountain of sins, and made a new man of him by the Holy Spirit.

Yang Chin-fu, for that was the farmer's name, listened to the very end; then slowly, as if in a dream, he rose and went home to Yuantsun. A new light which would never become extinguished had entered the man's soul. That evening Yang Chin-fu went into his great uncle's court next door and, signing to his great uncle's son-in- law, Dr. Chu, to come outside, the two seated, or, to be more exact, squatted themselves just within the shadow of the front entrance and ate their supper together. Each had a bowl of millet porridge which he poised on one hand, while chopsticks in the other served for cutlery. As they ate, Yang Chin-fu told the other of his visit to the foreign compound and of what he had heard. He spoke in a low voice, so that others might not hear, and begged Dr. Chu to accompany him to hear for himself the following day. Dr. Chu listened sympathetically and with real interest and agreed to go. To tell in detail of what followed and of the growth of the light in that center would make a long and interesting story which cannot now be told; sufficient to say the outcome of their visit was that both became Christians and before a year had passed most of the great Yang clan either had come out publicly for Christ or were secret believers.

2. YANG YU-MING, THE SERVANT

What I have written thus far has been by way of introducing my reader to the Yang family, for from now on my story must follow just one member of it, Yang Yu-ming, the younger nephew of the farmer mentioned above. The father of this boy had been a very bad man. Among other crimes laid to his account were highway robbery and murder. When Christ entered this man's heart the old life was left behind, for from the time of his conversion till his death, a few years later, as far as we knew he lived a consistent Christian life.

Yu-ming, the younger of his two sons, was one of our first schoolboys. He attended the mission school for about three years, then, because of the death of his father and the extreme poverty of the family (his father having long before gambled away his share of the family property), the boy was obliged to leave school and seek employment. One of our newly arrived missionaries took him on as a servant. Our only remembrance of Yu-ming at this time was that he made a nice, clean-looking servant for Mr. Griffith. He served thus for barely two years, when, like a clap of thunder, the Boxer uprising came upon us in all its cataclysm of horror. Missionaries and converts were scattered far and wide, hunted down like wild beasts, hundreds throughout China being done to death by the merciless Boxers.

Not a few of our converts made their way out to the coast, Yu-ming being among these. He begged and tramped his way many hundreds of miles right through the heart of the Boxer country, enduring great perils and hardships, but at last reached Weihaiwei, a Chinese port on the coast under the control of the British. Many British soldiers were stationed there from England and India, the latter being called Sikhs. We know almost nothing of Yu-ming life at this port except that he formed a friendship with a Christian Sikh soldier. This man had a wonderful influence over Yu-ming for good. Through him the young lonely boy, so far away from home and friends, was led to give himself in a new way to the Lord. The reality of the change which at this time came over Yu- ming was shown by a letter which he wrote to his former master. In this letter he confessed many things and begged for forgiveness. He told of his new-found friend and of the great change and blessing which had come to him. (How often we wished we could have come to know more about this faithful Indian servant of Christ whose influence reached so far in after years!)

More than a year passed and the missionaries began to return to their stations and affairs were rapidly becoming normal. As servant to Mr. Slimmon Yu-ming joined one of the parties returning to Honan, and accompanied him to the mission station of Hwaikingfu. His new master very soon saw that in Yu-ming which convinced him the boy, or rather the now tall, fully developed young man, had in him possibilities far above his position as a servant, and finally offered to use his influence to obtain a position for him in the Chinese post office. This in time was secured, though Yu-ming had to enter his "official" position on the very lowest rung of the ladder, some of his tasks being of the most menial kind. To get in to the post office at all he needed to know not a little English, both written and spoken, and Yu-ming gratefully acknowledged that he owed all he knew along these lines to the patient teaching of his faithful friend, the Christian Sikh.

The young man did not stay long on the lowest rung of the ladder, as we shall now see.

3. CLIMBING THE LADDER

One day when I was busy at one end of our long bungalow house a message came from my husband that a visitor waited in his study to see me. Meeting my husband outside the door, I tried to get him to say who the visitor was, but he would not. I was therefore quite unprepared to see a tall, fine-looking young man with soldierly bearing, well-dressed and with the manners and speech of a refined gentleman. I looked again and again, puzzled, while my husband stood by, smiling; then a little something of the old Yu-ming revealed who it was. But, oh, how unlike was he to the uncouth servant lad we parted from in 1900! But it was truly delightful, as we talked together, to find an entire absence of that up-startishness which we had feared to find in him. Instead there was a quiet, humble dignity in his manner and in what he said which deeply impressed us, and we soon perceived the secret of this lay in his sincere, devout Christian spirit. Before he left we knelt and my husband committed him into the hands of his higher Master (he was to begin his duties in the post office the following day). As we rose, Yu-ming quietly said:

"Of all that the Lord enables me to earn I promise to give Him a tithe." Who can say how much this honouring of God in his life had to do with his after success, for is it not written, "He that honoureth Me I will honour?"

For several years we saw very little of Mr. Yang, as he now came to be called; but we heard of him, for his rapid rise from one position to another, ever higher in the scale of the postal service, became the wonder of all. Mr. Yang early attracted the attention of the foreign postal inspector from Peking, and in course of time a warm friendship sprang up between these two. As time passed the inspector showed in many practical ways his esteem and affection for his young subordinate. Mr. Yang owed much, undoubtedly, to this friendship.

Although we had watched with something akin to wonder Yu-ming's, or we should say Mr. Yang's, rapid advancement, we were scarcely prepared to hear one day that he had been appointed to the position of postmaster at the large, important city of Weihuifu, a few hours' run by rail south of Changte, at a salary of at least twenty times that which he had received as servant to the missionary.

The time had come when his marriage was thought advisable by his parents and the parents of the girl who had been chosen for him when he was a boy of ten and the girl two years younger, I would gladly pass over this part of the story, for I never can recall it without a heartsick feeling coming over me. But it lifts the veil a little from the cruel, unjust marriage customs which prevail in China.

Had Mr. Yang remained a servant and what he was when he was a servant, his marriage to the girl chosen for him would not have been out of the way. But he had not. He had gone on mentally and spiritually and in tastes and habits far, far beyond what the girl had remained. I felt so sorry that this splen-did young fellow's life and happiness should be wrecked on a cruel, unjust custom that I ventured to approach the parties concerned and suggested that the girl be betrothed to one of her own station and Mr. Yang be permit-ted to choose his own bride. But this suggestion meant the overturning of age-crystallized customs, and the very suggestion brought down upon me such a storm of protest from the Chinese I dropped the matter like a hot coal.

The marriage took place. Shortly afterwards, Mr. Yang's mother escorted the bride to his home at Weihuifu, and remained there, for it would never have done to allow a young bride out of the safe care and keeping of her mother-in-law! Before the reader can form any idea as to what that short-lived home life must have meant to our young friend, Mr. Yang, it is necessary that you should know something of his mother.

How can I describe her? Of all the Yang family, the religion of Jesus Christ seemed to change her the least. Her rough, coarse, nagging voice grated on one's every nerve. Yet when one thinks of those years of grinding poverty, with little ones to feed, and only her mother instinct to keep her toiling from daylight till midnight; half-starved and her children ever looking to her for food, while her opium-smoking husband stole from the home everything he could lay his hands on; when, I say, we think of these things, who of us dares criticize her too severely? Thank God, the Judge of men knows all when judging, not only the paltry surface things by which we mortals judge.

We must, therefore, take old Mrs. Yang as we find her and try to picture the home life Yang Yu-ming had— the only real home life of his own he was ever permitted to have. But perhaps it was just as well it was not for long. The postal authorities picked upon him to fill a still higher post. This time he was appointed to be inspector of post-offices for the whole of the important Province of Honan. This work required constant travel, so mother and bride were sent back to the old home at Yuantsun.

Mr. Yang now received a salary about *thirty* times what he had received as a servant a few years before. Whether he kept strictly to his promise to give the Lord a tithe I cannot say. But the missionaries at Weihuifu told me he always gave generously to the church there, and his old home church at Changte received frequent generous gifts from him. His home folks, too, were not forgotten. The old tumbled-down houses in the home courts at Yuantsun were rebuilt, and one quite new two-roomed brick cottage was built for his bride, but it is doubtful if he ever lived in it.

How long Mr. Yang remained as inspector I do not recall, but it could not have been more than a year or so. Then the last and still higher post was offered him. For a long time the postal authorities in Peking had been looking out for a man to send into the distant far-reaching province of Sinkiang. A glance at a map of China will show this province reaching for hundreds of miles far to the northwest. To plant postal stations throughout this vast territory required a man of great courage and strength of character. It needed above all a man that could be trusted. Yang Yu-ming was asked to undertake the difficult mission. When he received the call, he calmly accepted the trust in the spirit which had won for him such golden opinions from the time of his first entering the service.

His preparations were soon made and the long, difficult, and dangerous journey of many months began. No steamboat or rail helped by the way, but hardships and difficulties were met with all along (this I know so well after years of like travel in China). Months passed, and then word came of his safe arrival, and later we heard of the good service he was doing.

A bright light on his life as a Christian at this time was shed unexpectedly just as I was about to close this sketch. When traveling by train we met a missionary, and in course of conversation I mentioned the fact of my writing about one of our Christians, and one or two facts given led this missionary to turn quickly to me and ask:

"Do you mean Yang Yu-ming?"

"Yes," I replied. "But do you know about him?"

"I should think I do," returned the missionary. "I was stationed in a lonely mission center many days' journey from any other mission station far into the Province of Sinkiang. Then to my great joy, as I found out the worth of the man, Mr. Yang arrived and made my station his headquarters. From the first he helped me in every possible way. When I had to leave the station for a tour into the country, Mr. Yang took control for me, leading Sunday services and whatever needed to be done. One of the last messages he left with me before he passed away concerned certain monies he wished given to the church in Honan, as he considered he owed on his tithe." The missionary then spoke with deep feeling of what it had meant to him to have Mr. Yang's fellowship and sympathy in that lonely place.

But the Master's call to come up higher came to this faithful servant a little more than a year after reaching his distant field. After a short sharp struggle with hemorrhage of the lungs, he passed away. News of his death reached Peking by telegraph. The postal authorities at once telegraphed for the body to be brought back to his home in Yuantsun. It mattered not to them that this must of necessity entail great expenditure of money. Neither did they spare any expense on the arrival of the body, but they did everything to show honor to the one whom everyone mourned as a friend or as one who had influenced his life for the highest; for Mr. Yang's life had shown as had the lives of few others the transforming and keeping power of his Great Master.

Nor was this all. The postal authorities gave to the mother and widow a sufficient sum of money to insure for them a life support. With this the land which had been gambled away by the father in the old heathen days was repurchased.

VI. CAMEOS OF ONE CHINESE VILLAGE

1. WINNING A WOULD-BE MURDERER

"Only like souls I see the folk thereunder,

Bound! who should conquer; Slaves! who should be kings;

Hearing their one hope with an empty wonder,

Sadly contented with a show of things,"

ONE DAY as Dr. Goforth was preaching in the street chapel in Changte city, he noticed a bright, intelligent-looking young man listening with keen attention.

SCRIPTURE TESTIMONY
Believers will suffer terrible things for the sake of Jesus' name
MATTHEW 24:9-14

Speaker after speaker gave his message, and the missionary from his place on the platform watched with interest the evident signs of mental awakening on the young man's face. At the close of the meeting the visitor was greeted cordially and invited back to the evangelist's room for further instruction.

Two days later saw the young man, Chang-san by name, on his way home to the village of Hsiwen, ten miles north of the city of Changte. His heart was filled with fear, for he knew his father's ungovernable temper, which had earned for him the name of "The Fury." He knew, only too well, his father's bitter hatred of the missionaries and anything savoring of the foreigner. "But," the young man said to himself, "am I not now a Christian? Did I not openly confess Jesus Christ as my Saviour only last night in the street chapel before all the crowd gathered there?" And as he thought on these things a feeling akin to panic seized him, and as his home came in sight he looked up and cried aloud an agonized prayer for help, "O God! O my Saviour! I have no strength. Help me." He remembered the missionary's last words, "Your first step in your new life must be to confess Christ before your own people," and before the village was reached Chang-san had determined at all costs he would confess the Lord Jesus.

He had not been home many days before all began to remark that something was the matter with the boy. "Why," they said, "he does not even take trouble or time to curse the chickens that get in his way." The poor fellow went about pale, nervous, and silent. He tried to meet inquiries by evasive replies, but at last, as if unable to contain himself longer, he threw himself down on the brick floor before his father and burst into a passion of weeping, knocking his head again and again on the bricks at his father's feet.

The old man demanded an explanation, but feared nothing worse than some young man's escapade in the city, and of course this would be lightly passed over. When the father said as much, Chang-san seemed to gain control of himself and, rising, stood before his father.

"No, father," he said, "it is not what you think. I have nothing to regret. Father, listen! I am now a Christian and I weep because you do not understand. I heard the missionary in Changte tell the wonderful story how…" But he could get no further, for the father, springing to his feet, in a passion of rage seized him by the collar, then striking, pushing, and kicking, forced him out through the court, up a narrow lane, on to the street. Like a wind passing over the village, the news spread, "a row at the Chang's home," which brought a great crowd in high glee to see the fun of a family fight!

As the father kicked and struck his son unmercifully, as if to drive the demons out of him, he kept shouting, "The foreigner has bewitched him." Chang-san made no attempt to strike back, but sought only to defend himself as best he could from the blows rained upon him. The old father, when almost spent, stopped for breath and cried: "Will you recant? Will you curse the foreigner?" But Chang-san remaining obdurate, the father became quite beyond himself. Pale with fury, he rushed for his own gateway, shouting: "A hatchet! A hatchet! I'll kill him!" No one dared try to stop him, and all knew the old man well enough to fear he meant indeed to murder his son. But as soon as the demented old "Fury" disappeared, a number of the leading men of the village rushed Chang-san off to a neighbor's home and hid him. The crowd, now realizing that this family fight was more than "fun," quickly disappeared behind barred gates.

That night, under cover of darkness, Chang-san made his way back to the mission gate, which he reached just as it was being closed for the night. Kind evangelists gave him shelter and sympathy. The following day a "council of war" was held in Dr. Goforth's study, and it was decided that a peace delegation should go to Hsiwen, give the village a day's preaching, and endeavor to see the father.

To give the history of that day would be to tell a story in itself. In brief, the party received at first a scant, cold welcome from the villagers. No one offered to bring them a bench to rest upon after their long ten-mile dusty walk, nor, as usual, a table for their books; but they just stood their ground and began preaching. To say the least it was most discouraging for more than an hour to see groups of villagers squatting by their doors, smoking and chatting about their strange visitors, but all keeping just out of hearing, except, indeed, a crowd of ungovernable shouting children and barking dogs. As a last hope of drawing an audience, hymn books were passed around and "Jesus loves me" started up. The effect was beyond what any had dared to hope, for before the third verse was reached a fair-sized company had gathered, and from then till they left they were never without listeners. Soon a table was brought and two benches, and as the hours passed a teapot filled with hot water, and several tiny bowls, were placed for their use.

Even though Dr. Goforth had sent his card in to Chang-san's father with the request to be allowed to call, the old man made no sign of having even received the card. All day the poor old "Fury" sat in his home, nursing his anger and refusing to listen to the favorable reports which neighbors kept bringing in of the foreigner. "He had a kind, good face," one reported; another said, "All his words were according to *li*"—i.e., right reason.

At last the missionary patience became exhausted. "I'm going to see him whether he wants me to or not." But Chinese children have quick ears and quicker feet, and a few moments after the above remark had passed the missionary's lips a boy came rushing in where Chang-san's father sat and whispered to him, "The foreigner is coming." The old man, without taking time to put on his outer garment, ran out through the back gate, and never stopped till he was safely hidden in a near-by village.

One can better imagine than describe the missionary's feelings when he found the old man had run away. He had, however, the satisfaction of being received by the rest of the Chang family, all of whom gathered about him while he preached unto them the unsearchable riches of Christ. Not till the shadows lengthened did the party turn their faces homeward.

A few days later one of our most trusted evangelists, Mr. Ho (by trade an idol-maker before his conversion), was intrusted with the task of accompanying Chang-san back to his home. When the old father heard that his son, accompanied by another man, was coming up the village street, he seized a large iron poker, similar to those used in large furnaces, and, rushing out, attempted to strike his son over the head. But Mr. Ho was too quick for him. Striking the poker aside, he seized the old man's wrists with an iron grip. Struggle and fume as he would, Mr. Ho held on until he forced the promise from the old "Fury" that he would not again attempt to do his son bodily harm.

During the months which followed several of the leading men in the village came out as Christians, and one by one every member of Chang-san's own family decided for Christ. The old father was the last to yield, but when he did he became a power for good, for the villagers *saw* the great change which Christ wrought in him, making the once much-feared old "Fury" a peaceable, kindly neighbor.

Before the old man's last call came he rejoiced to see both of his sons catch such a vision of the need for Christ among the millions around them that they gave themselves to the work of evangelism. The old father rejoiced too, more and more, as the end drew near, that the Gospel of salvation from sin and a hope after death had come to his village not too late to save a great sinner such as he knew himself to be.

Thus the standard of the Cross was first set up in the village of Hsiwen.

2. HOW "OLD AUTOCRAT" WAS WON BY A SKETCH

What a cross, crabbed old creature she was! Her face looked like a piece of crinkled brown paper with two little sharp black eyes looking you through and through. No wonder she was called the "Old Autocrat" because for over twenty years she had exercised unique authority as senior woman of the entire Chang clan, whose numbers were legion. What the exact relationship was between Chang-san and this old lady I never could quite puzzle out. It was about as complicated as that of our old hostess at a certain place, who said she was related to one of our evangelists. Curious to know what the relationship was, I pressed her for it and, not being able to remember it correctly five minutes after, I wrote it down. This is what she said: *"Paifang ti nai nai shih zvo Chang fu ti tieh ti ku ku"*. This being exactly translated is, "Pai fang's grandmother was my husband's father's brother's daughter!"

Within old Mrs. Chang's own court were three small buildings, each facing into the court; it was in the south building where this curious old character had lived a widow and alone for twenty years. It was here she kept carefully guarded all her earthly treasures. And such treasures! Crocks of every size and degree of imperfection, some emitting far from pleasant odors; baskets from which old shoe soles protruded, with bits of all kinds of scraps, etc.; broken boards and pieces of useless furniture filled every crevice between the crocks. The only place which ever seemed cleared was the *kang* (brick platform bed) in the little inner room. Neatly folded quilts of brilliant colors were always in evidence, while the *kang* itself was covered with a neat straw mat. Immediately in front of the *kang* was a tiny brick stove with a flue which carried the heat under the hollow kang. How many times have I felt the comfort and warmth of these warm bricks after a cold ten-mile cart-ride in winter!

Just outside her bedroom window the old woman kept her own coffin. It had rested there for twenty years, so as to be safely guarded against thieves.

Yes, she was indeed a real character. Every time we visited the village she would take refuge in this treasure-house of hers, closely barring the door lest she meet the foreign woman and become contaminated.

One day when Dr. Goforth and I were spending the week-end preaching at Hsiwen, Chang-san's mother said to me: "I do wish we could win the 'Old Autocrat'. She is making it so hard for us Christians. Everyone fears her tongue, and so keeps in with her. She just hates us Christians." As she spoke, a sudden thought struck me.

"Mrs. Wang," I said to my dear Bible woman, in whom I had complete confidence, "you go over to old Mrs. Chang's door and see if you can get in touch with her while we remain here and pray for you." Off Mrs. Wang went as quickly as her poor crippled feet could carry her. Arriving at the "Old Autocrat's" door she knocked once, twice, three times, but no response came. Mrs. Wang knew the old lady was within, for the bar was fastened inside. Just as she was about to turn away a faint sound of the bar being drawn could be heard. Then very slowly the two-leafed door opened just a little.

"What do you want?" came gruffly from inside.

"I just want to come and pay my respects to you, venerable grandmother," replied Mrs. Wang, sweetly.

"I know what you have come for-just to talk against my gods!" was the sharp retort.

"No, indeed," said Mrs. Wang, quickly. "I'll not say a word about your gods. I'll only talk about mine if you let me in."

This seemed to please the old woman, and opening the door a little further she said: "Well, if you promise not to speak against my gods I'll let you in."

So Mrs. Wang promised, the door opened, and in she went. I have often laughed to myself at the highly colored picture Mrs. Wang must have drawn of me to the poor old body, for it was not long before she became curious to see the foreign woman for herself. At last she asked:

"Do you think she would come over if I were to invite her?"

Scarcely able to hide her elation, Mrs. Wang replied, "I think she would if I went for her."

A few moments later we were all startled by Mrs. Wang bursting breathlessly into our midst. "Do come at once, the old woman has invited you over!"

We all started off in haste, and on arriving at the old woman's door I was surprised at the warmth of my reception. Inborn fear was very evidently struggling with equally inborn courtesy, and the latter won out as she placed me on the least rickety bench. Almost immediately the old lady opened fire.

"Do you mean to tell me those eyes do not see me?" pointing to a hideous contorted picture representing the god of wealth which occupied the place of honor on the wall immediately opposite the door. Feeling the need for going very carefully with this strange old character, I replied:

"Do you really think they *can* see you?"

"Of course they can! And those and those," said the "Old Autocrat," pointing to several other minor gods hanging on the wall. Before replying I raised my heart in a cry for wisdom, and then said:

"Venerable grandmother, do you think I can make eyes that can see?"

"You certainly cannot" she replied, emphatically.

"Do you think I could make a god?" I again asked.

"You most certainly cannot," still more emphatically.

"Then," I said, "if I make eyes that *seem* to look at you far more really than those of any of these gods, and I make them on paper like the gods are printed on, will you, my venerable grandmother, believe that these eyes which you *think* can see you are only picture eyes that *seem* to see?"

For several moments we faced each other, looking straight into each other's eyes, while the crowd waited with bated breath. Then the old woman tossed her head, and with a laugh as of victory said, "Ah, but you can't do it!"

"You just see," I cried, quickly. "Wait here and I will be back in a few moments." Away I flew through the courts, gates, and alleys over to Chang-san's home, where we were staying. Dr. Goforth was reading his Bible on the *kang* by the window.

"Oh, be quick, Jonathan," I cried, "and get me a red and a blue pencil, a fountain pen, a lead and an indelible pencil." While he was gathering these together I told him what I was about to do, and catching up a large unruled writing pad and the pencils, I hastened back.

The crowd had greatly increased, and the room was so packed I could scarcely get elbow room.

"Now," I said, "you must not touch my arm and you must give me light." I made room for the "Old Autocrat" beside me, and there she stood through it all, watching every line I drew. Many years before as a girl my dear father had taught me to draw the outlines of a human face by rule, and I determined to follow these rules. As my pencils flew, the interest increased, till the crowd just swayed back and forth in their effort to see what I was drawing. With the red pencil I colored the cheeks and lips, with the blue the eyes and dress were tinted, and black curly hair was made with the fountain pen. But the final touches to the eyes I reserved to the last, and as I was doing this I prayed that the Lord might enable me to make them very lifelike. When the last touch was finished I felt almost startled myself, for the eyes seemed to look so at one.

"Oh, give it to me, give it to me!" cried the "Old Autocrat," trying to snatch the picture from me.

"No, no," I replied. "I cannot give it to you unless you promise not to worship it." Then making my way through the crowd to where the god of wealth hung, I held my picture up beside the contorted face of the god and said to the "Old Autocrat," who had followed me:

"Now, venerable grandmother, tell me truthfully which pair of eyes *seem* to look at you the best?" The old woman was silent for several moments while a great stillness reigned in the room. Then with a big sigh and a catch in her voice and a look in her eyes that was half frightened and half awakened, she stretched out her hand, begging: .

"Say no more, lady. Give me the picture and I'll promise not to worship it." I saw the poor old body had been under great strain and thought it wisest to say no more. The old woman's face was a study as she looked at the picture I had just drawn. One of the women in the crowd called out:

"I guess you don't know, lady, what a *hao chao hua ti* old grandmother is!" The Chinese being freely translated means "a connoisseur in art!"

"Oh, you are?" I said, turning to the old woman. "Then we will be great friends, for I am quite a connoisseur in art, too! I have lots of pictures, and every time I come up from Changte I'll try and remember to bring you one."

In the months that followed, many a brilliant picture torn from *The Ladies' Home Journal* or other papers found their way on to the "Old Autocrat's" walls and gradually replaced the execrable pictures which had won her reputation as a collector of art!

The great change of heart came slowly with this strange yet lovable old woman. Long before we could be sure she had a personal love for the Lord Jesus as her Saviour she had become devoted to Dr. Goforth and myself. Indeed, long before we were satisfied that the old woman's heart was changed (for, sad to say, the villagers still had reason to fear her tongue) she had become a great blessing to the church and especially to the Christian women. One of her houses just across the court from where she lived was rented to the Christians as a chapel and schoolhouse. Her court became the rendezvous for the Christian women before and between Sunday service. At such times the old lady gave herself up to keeping the women supplied with hot water to drink, and in other ways seeking to make them feel at home.

As time passed the old woman seemed to lose her fear of her coffin being stolen, and had it removed from under her bedroom window to a place beside the preacher's desk in the chapel, where for years it made a convenient stand for the congregation Bibles and hymn-books. The first time I saw it there, I said to the evangelist in charge, "Surely you are not going to allow *that thing* to stay there!" He replied, "Why not, lady? It's empty!" Not being able to say just "why," there the coffin remained! Not long before leaving China for furlough old Mrs. Chang (for I do not like to call her the "Old Autocrat" any longer) said to me, "I'm coming down to Changte to see you." I expressed my delight at the prospect of a visit. A few weeks later the old woman, now over eighty, appeared at our door. What a delight she took in examining everything from the kitchen stove to the globe in Dr. Goforth's study! But it was the pictures which seemed to fascinate her; again and again she turned to them. As we stood together looking at a beautiful picture of snow-clad Rocky Mountain peaks which my brother had painted and given me years before, I saw a strange and to me beautiful wistfulness on the old woman's face, and the thought of the chrysalis came to me, how it was shut up in its unlovely hard crust till the moment of its deliverance. So I thought, this old woman with her instinctive love for the beautiful has been for eighty years inclosed, imprisoned, in the hard unbroken crust of a heathen environment; but the grace of God has begun the change within and the moment of her souls deliverance is at hand when she can come forth unfettered and beautified to ascend to the God who made her. Who knows, dear reader, but that one day you may meet the once "Old Autocrat"" but then a beautified soul changed into His image in the Gloryland?

3. LITTLE MARY AND THE SMALLPOX BABIES

"There shall be no evil befall thee,

neither shall any plague come nigh

thy dwelling."

SCRIPTURE TESTIMONY
As we serve Him, the Lord will be our defense
LUKE 10:19 · 2 THESSALONIANS 3:1-3

When taking my Bible women for a day's preaching in the village of which I am now writing, I rarely allowed any of the children to accompany us, knowing too well the danger from infectious diseases. Epidemics of one kind or another were of frequent occurrence. But one day as we were about to start for a day at village, my faithful old nurse, Mrs. Cheng, and said: "Do take Mary with you. I can manage the others if she is not here." So hurriedly we dressed our little five-year-old auburn-haired lassie and our springless two-wheeled cart. For three hours we bumped over the rough roads, and glad I was when the village of Hsiwen came in sight; but Mary's spirits seemed to rise with every jolt, for it was to her only a delightful picnic.

We were cordially received by the Chang women, and taken into the same room where Chang-san had knelt before his old father. Rain coming on, we were prevented from preaching as usual in the open court, so a place was cleared on the great platform-bed for Mary and myself and the Bible women, while the crowd packed both the room we were in and on through the adjoining room out to the court itself. There was only one small window, and the room, even on a bright day, was so dark one could not make out clearly the faces and forms of those beyond a few feet, All day the crush continued and everyone wanted to see the little foreign child *with colored hair!* What a time we had trying to get a hearing for our message, for so many pressed on us to feel as well as see Mary and everything on her. My Bible woman, Mrs. Wang, and I took turns in preaching to the crowd. By late afternoon we were thoroughly tired out.

All through the day Mrs. Chang-san was most attentive to us, bringing food cooked by herself and replenishing again and again the hot-water bowls. I was so much engaged with trying to keep order, and guard Mary, and preach myself, that I only casually noticed that Mrs. Chang-san had a baby wrapped inside her wadded garment. The child was so covered I could not see its face.

At noon Mrs. Chang-san brought a tray of steaming bowls of dough-strings and garlic. Mary and the Bible women seemed to greatly enjoy this repast, while the crowd watched with keen delight the foreign child's manipulation of the chopsticks, for she was able to use them much more dexterously than her mother.

As the hours passed and it came near time for us to leave, the air in the room became almost overpowering. It was then I first noticed several women back in the crowd with babies in their arms, all of whom had white cloths over their faces. A feeling of sick horror came over me, for I knew what a white cloth on a baby's face meant. *Smallpox!* I knew then from past experiences there must be an epidemic of smallpox in the village. Just then Mrs. Chang-san came in, and I quickly pulled aside her garment and looked at the baby inside. It was what I feared—the child's face was a mass of putrid scabs.

"Oh, Mrs. Chang-san," I cried, "why did you not warn me? Just think of the danger to little Mary!"

"Oh, lady," she replied, "it is really of no matter! Don't you know *all* children should have the smallpox, for they will grow up stronger *if they live!*"

Seeing the uselessness of arguing and realizing the importance of getting Mary outside as speedily as possible, we hastily said farewell and departed. On the way home little Mary wondered why mother hugged her so closely, and little did she realize how mother's heart was filled with a sickening fear. Many times the cry arose, "O God, keep my children from this dread disease."

For weeks I took Mary's temperature and felt her head many times a day, but no smallpox developed, and in spite of my lack of faith the Lord kept the disease from us. Later I found that Mary's visit to Hsiwen did wonders in opening the hearts of the heathen women and in removing much of their opposition towards us. It was the "touch of nature which makes the whole world kin" that had opened their hearts.

4. THE GAMBLER'S END

Now is the accepted time. Now is the day of salvation.

One of the greatest social evils of China is gambling. It is universal. In many men it amounts to a passion. In such cases the habit is as hard to overcome as the cravings of the

> SCRIPTURE TESTIMONY
>
> *There is no sting in death for the believer*
>
> I CORINTHIANS 15:54-57

opium fiend. We have known men to gamble away lands and property, wife and children. Such a man was Chang, the breadmaker of Hsiwen, who belonged to the same family and clan as those written of in the previous sketches. He was one of the most inveterate gamblers of the village, and but for his hard-working little wife the family would have fared badly. As it was, all the land that they had once possessed was gambled away.

The family consisted of the father, mother, and one daughter married and living in a village nearby, and two boys, aged twelve and fourteen. Their court lay between Chang-san's and the "Old Autocrat's." As we went from one of these to the other we must, needs pass down a narrow alley which led by the gambler's door. Many times as we turned down this alley the gambler's family could be seen on their doorstep, but on catching sight of us they would immediately go inside and close the door. Oh, how often had I longed to reach them with the Gospel! But in such cases one could only wait for God to open a way. This He did, but not as I expected.

The daughter becoming very ill, Chinese doctors pricked and punctured her till one wondered how she lived; and when, more dead than alive, the poor girl was carried over to her father's home, for the first time the gambler and his wife allowed some of their Christian neighbors to visit them, for they soon found the Christians were the only ones who could offer comfort in the face of probable death.

The sick girl and her mother both responded eagerly to the message of redeeming love, their stricken hearts being opened to any ray of hope. But the father, while not opposing and even at times apparently interested enough to listen, went on his old way, gambling day and night.

Soon it became apparent that if the sick girl's life was to be saved she must be taken to Dr. Dow's woman's hospital at Changte. Even the heathen husband's relations consented to this, so mother and daughter went to Changte. A very large internal tumor had to be removed, and warning was clearly given that there was only a slim chance of recovery. Dr. Goforth and I were leaving for a country town the day before the operation was to take place and I shall not forget the look of absolute peace and even joy on the face of the poor girl as I bade her good-by.

"Do not fear for me," she said as she clung to my hand. "I am so happy. I know that I will go to Jesus if I die, so why should I fear?"

Dr. Leslie assisted in the operation, and for several nights Dr. Dow slept in the hospital beside the patient in order to be within a moment's call. The girl came through safely. For many weeks she and her mother remained in the hospital, hearing and seeing many things which strengthened their faith and opened their eyes to what the missionaries really were. On their return home the daughter became a living wonder to all; and, oh, how she just overflowed with praises and thanksgiving for what had been done and for the love and kindness shown them.

The gambling father could not but be touched by all this, and for a time Dr. Goforth and the evangelists had hopes of winning him. One

SCRIPTURE TESTIMONY
Don't put off the decision for salvation
ACTS 24:25 ·
2 CORINTHIANS 6:2 · JAMES 4:14

New-year's season, when the whole village was given up to holiday-making and vice was at its worst, Dr. Goforth went up for the Sunday services. Meeting Chang, the gambler, on the street, he again pleaded with him not to delay, but to give himself to the Lord. He quoted a common saying of the Chinese, "When you take your shoes and socks at night, who knows if you will ever put them on again." But the man only laughed, and as he walked on said over his shoulder, "I'll be a Christian some day, but not now; this is the special gambling season." A strange fear for the man so took possession of Dr. Goforth that he said to one of the evangelists: "I'm afraid for that man. He knows the truth and is practically challenging God to await his time. Try and get an opportunity to plead with him again."

That afternoon the evangelist went to the gambler's home and in every way sought to bring him to immediate decision, but failed. The same evening the gambler said to his family: "I'm strong and well. What's there to fear? I'll gamble till the fifteenth of the next moon, and then I'll quit."

He was a man in the prime of life, tall, strongly built, and apparently in the best of health. He took his supper as usual with his family, and then walked out. Passing down the village street in the dark, he went on until he came to the first gambling-den on the outskirts of the village—a dugout with straw roof, similar in construction to a vegetable-pit. Here he joined the ring of gamblers already playing. For an hour he played, steadily losing. Hoping for better luck elsewhere, he went out into the darkness to a second gambling-den nearby. Feeling his way down into the pit, he was about to take his place in the ring when his arms flew up and he sank to the ground —a lifeless body.

What saith the Scriptures?—"Take thine ease, eat, drink, and be merry. But God said unto him, Thou fool, this night thy soul shall be required of thee." (Luke 12: 20)

5. THE OLD VIOLINIST

As the years flew by Christians were gathered not only from the village of Hsiwen itself, but also from many of the surrounding villages. The chapel in the "Old Autocrat's" court became too small to hold the Sunday congregations. The little room adjoining the chapel where the teacher and evangelist slept was often filled with women and children during public services, and many had even to sit out in the courtyard. It was probably the pressing need for room, combined with public opinion, that succeeded in ousting the old woman's coffin from its place beside the preacher's desk. The hymn-books and Bibles, no longer having the coffin for a resting-place, were piled on the window-sill.

Whenever Dr. Goforth and I had a Sunday to spare it was a delight to take a run up to this center. A happy, hearty crowd of Christians were always at the gate to welcome us with that love light in their eyes never seen on a heathen face. Before and between meetings the women crowded about the "Old Autocrat's" door, filling porch, steps, and many sitting on the brick court. Each one brought her own piece of bread for noon lunch, old Mrs. Chang providing hot water to drink. I do not recall hearing these women gossip, but all studied diligently at hymn-book, catechism, or Bible, according to the progress made, those more advanced helping the beginners.

While there was much to cheer and encourage us at this center, there was one thing which had always given me pain, and that was the congregational singing! The Christians very early seemed to get into most hopeless ruts, each one apparently singing quite independently as to time and key, and some as to tune. The most we could give them was a very occasional Sabbath, and we knew that only an occasional "boost" is not sufficient to get a large firmly fixed body out of a rut. Many times I have stopped the singing and given the key note, telling them all to listen and start at a given sign. Temporary improvement could be discernible, but on our return a few months later they were deeper than ever in the old ruts.

Then came several years absence when we were on furlough and filling gaps elsewhere. On our return Hsiwen was one of the first places visited. A surprise awaited us. It seemed that an old musician living in a near-by village had become a Christian during our absence. He had offered his services, we were told, as leader of music for the congregation, and was accepted! On this first visit after our return, for some reason I did not bring my organ with me, and so decided to sit to one side with the women and watch proceedings.

Dr. Goforth had taken his place at the table and the congregation was settling down to quiet, when in walked very slowly the old musician. His ragged clothes plainly revealed he belonged to that great always hungry class which we met with everywhere in China. Under his arm was the queerest violin. He had made it himself of split bamboo. Indeed, it resembled a violin in little else than that it was worked by a string bow on three or four cords or violin strings. The old musician took his seat on a bench just where the coffin had rested for years. He had an air of dignity which seemed to bespeak his consciousness of the honor put upon him. Slowly he began to draw his bow across the string. Oh, how can I describe the result? The sounds which came from the poor, fragile, quivering violin, which seemed about to fall to pieces each moment, reminded me of my childhood's greatest horror - when my neighbor at school would scrape on the slate with a brittle pencil for the pleasure of witnessing my agony! It sounded as if the bow were being drawn back and forth on the one string and on the same spot. Then he stopped suddenly. I suppose he had been tuning up!

Dr. Goforth gave out the hymn, whereupon the violinist repeated as near as I could make out just what he had performed before. While I was straining my ears to discover the tune, the congregation commenced singing and in the same old way, each for him or her self. The only addition was the old musician, who scraped quite independently notes at least half an octave higher than any voice could reach.

I looked at my husband, but his face was as grave as a judge's. Glancing around to see if anyone else saw the funny side of it all, I found everyone singing with great enjoyment, the rapt look on their faces revealing a spirit of true worship within. Ashamed, I turned my eyes back to my hymnbook and the lesson of "The Singing Monks" came to me. "Not the music from unworshipful lips, but the incense of praise from love-filled hearts, reaches the Majesty on High."

Our last visit to this center was a memorable one. During the four days of special meetings one hundred and two new believers came out on the Lord's side. The church at this center has for some time been self- supporting.

VII. THREE NOTABLE EVANGELISTS

I. A MILITARY MANDARIN

CAPTAIN LI-MING, commander of the AN YANG County militia, was a man of powerful physique. He had no real education, but was a man of dominating

SCRIPTURE TESTIMONY
Believers exchange supersti-tion for faith in Christ
ACTS 19:18-19

personality. He had three wives. In the eyes of many Chinese a man's greatness depends in measure upon the number of wives he has. When a new prefect once came to Changte, a Chinese friend, in speaking of this official, said that he had nine wives, and that seemed to be the most important thing he had to say of him. I remember the first time Captain Li heard the Gospel. We were preaching on the main street of Changte city and he listened for more than an hour. Later on he came and spent the evening with us, inquiring further, and bought a Christian catechism. Then for years we saw nothing more of him. On our moving to Changte permanently, he was often found in the audience. From what I learned from him later, he had lived, previous to his conversion, a very dissolute life.

The day that Captain Li finally decided, he said to me, "I am going home today to make an end of my household gods." The stern look on his face showed that he meant business. His home was in a village about two miles away. Arriving there, he told his wives what he was about to do. They were very much alarmed and pleaded with him not to provoke the gods. One of them slipped out and warned the friends and neighbors. Soon the compound was filled with friends pleading with him to desist. But Li was a man who, when he got an idea into his head, must carry it through. He tore all the gods down and brought them out into the center of the court. Opening the catechism where it said, "Thou shalt have no other gods before me," he applied a match to the pile and the gods went up in smoke. The shocked friends and neighbors went away, saying, "Within three days some dread happening will come down upon this offender." After three days, however, Li-ming was healthier and happier than ever, apparently, and they began to change their ideas.

When Li-ming, after months of added prosperity, seemed to have gained by the disposal of the gods, some of the people began to inquire of this New Way, and his three wives all turned to the Lord. Often have we heard Li-ming testifying about the trouble he used to have with those three wives.

"Sometimes," said he, "they would have a difference of opinion and get disputing, and then to reviling and pulling out one another's hair. At such times I would roar at them. If that was not sufficient, I laid on the horsewhip. Even then at times I could scarcely quiet them. But now the Lord Jesus has come into their hearts and taken possession of them, we have no more of the old quarrels, and I truly believe they love one another like three sisters."

Li-ming and his wives agreed to separate. One wife went to a distant city to be a Bible woman; another became assistant in one of the mission hospitals; the original wife remained at home. Li-ming became an efficient evangelist. He was willing to undergo any fatigue and hardship. When we had to travel over rough places with our barrow, I have seen that huge man wheeling the barrow with the perspiration pouring from him, or taking his turn helping to pull, as we all did. Some days we traveled twenty or twenty-five miles, and that on foot, and helping with the barrow, besides. After such a journey we naturally were all weary on arrival at the inn. The coming of a foreigner at an inn is always sure to attract an audience. It never was my custom to ask a Chinese evangelist to speak first, for they were always too weary and thirsty. Saying to the evangelists, "Sit down and drink tea," I would commence preaching. As soon as they were refreshed by a drink of tea, always one of them would come and urge me to rest and have tea also. In this way we were all kept in good humor.

Li-ming was invaluable as a preacher, for he himself was known all over the county. The very fact that he was now preaching this Gospel naturally stirred up a keen

SCRIPTURE TESTIMONY
Deliverance from enemies and circumstances
LUKE 1:71

interest everywhere. We have heard him repeatedly say that he saw the first opium pipe that came to Changte. Then it was a great curio. Since then it has become a curse.

"During the last thirty years" he would say, "I have seen more than half of the great wealthy families of Changte County go down to disaster through gambling, opium, and women."

Captain Li was a man of great faith. He believed that when God said anything He meant it, and that His promises surely could be relied upon. One year, when the wheat was just coming out in head, he was returning home, when he saw his neighbors all busy putting down little bannerettes and burning incense. They were running in a direction from southwest to northeast.

"What's up now?" asked Li.

The reply came: "Do you not know that the locusts are coming in great swarms from the southeast? We are sacrificing to the locust king, that he may head them off."

Li said: "This won't hinder them. They will come all the same, and eat your grain, too."

The neighbors replied: "Well, won't they eat yours when they come to eat ours, then?"

"No, they will not, for the God of Heaven whom I serve will hear my prayer and protect my grain."

"But," said the neighbors, "how are the locusts to distinguish? There are no walls or fences between our fields."

Li said: "I am not alarmed about that. My God will direct them." On came the locusts in vast swarms, devouring everything before them. Li had three different plots of grain. These were left untouched, while his neigh-bors, grain was all eaten. Each plot was left as Li had declared it would be. There was a poor Christian neighbor of his who had just one little field. The locusts never touched it, but ate everything around it.

Some time after this divine intervention I went with Li-ming and two other evangelists and preached in his own as well as in all the surrounding villages. In every place I would hear Li throw out the challenge:

"Do you not know how the God of Heaven heard my prayer and saved my grain and my Christian neighbor's from the locusts? Do you not know that my grain was all saved from them?"

"Yes."

"Was not all your grain devoured at that time?"

And again would come the "Yes." In every place I heard the people acknowledge that what he said was true.

I happened to use this as an illustration one Sunday evening in one of the large Presbyterian churches of Toronto. At the close the minister of the congregation protested:

"You never should have used that locust story in your address tonight, for Professor M… was in the audience. What do you suppose he would think of it?"

"Well," I asked, "is that incident any more wonderful than the divine interventions spoken of in the Old Testament?"

"No, I can't say that it is, but Professor M   says of those Old Testament miracles that they are unthinkable.,

In reply I said: "The Lord Jesus Christ has accepted them as genuine by putting His divine seal on that Old Testament. It matters not to me what any theological professor may think or say. I accept what Jesus Christ accepted."

A lady missionary from Shensi connected with the Swedish branch of the China Inland Mission related the following story before a body of missionaries at Kuling.

"In one of our country districts" she said, "there is a Christian of great faith. When the locusts came in swarms he stood in the center of his field and prayed to God to save his grain, The locusts ate everything of the neighbor's on the four sides; in fact, the whole countryside was left sere and bare. Even the foliage of the trees was eaten, but this man's grain was left unharmed." When this report was brought in, this lady said it seemed too wonderful to be true. Immediately she took a conveyance and went out to visit this man. True enough, there was a field of emerald green in the midst of a barren waste. This lady stated further that the heathen were so enraged at the locusts eating their grain and not the Christian's, they tried in every way to drive the pests into the Christian's grain, but their efforts were in vain, for the locusts would fly back into their faces.

It is a sorry state of affairs when professors think in the name of science their business is to undermine belief in the Word of God. We can't shut our eyes to the fact that this undermining has been done and is being done, and the present condition of the church and the world shows the appalling outcome.

Li-ming's faith was of the humble, child-like kind. He had no hesitation in accepting everything written in the Bible, and freely proclaimed it, as well as lived it. He died with a triumphant conviction that all was well.

2. A MODEL CONFUCIANIST
(Wang Shih-ying)

A short time after I had given my best evangelist, Wang-Mei, to Rev. John Griffith (mention of this is made in the sketch Nathanael), a noted scholar named Wang Shih-ying, whose home was some distance north of Changte, called to see me and have a talk over this Jesus doctrine that we were proclaiming everywhere.

For two hours I took this man through the Bible, giving him proof that in the plan of God the Father, in order to save lost men He must send His own Son to become man and die in the sinner's stead. I believe that day Mr. Wang went away a changed man.

From that time on he associated with us and with all those who were followers of the Lord Jesus Christ. After he was baptized a year later he came on as a learner, with a view to becoming an evangelist. He made most unusual progress in the study of the Bible. He took all that Jesus Christ said literally at its face value. The time he would spend at fasting and prayer for opium sots, gamblers, and friends whom he wanted to bring into the Kingdom put all of us to shame.

On one occasion he visited one of our large mission centers. The evangelists there received him joyfully and prepared a feast for him. He refused to partake of it, saying: "I understand that you evangelists are not loving one another as your Saviour commanded you. Your enmity against one another is grieving the Holy Spirit and hindering the salvation of souls. I cannot eat your food. I must spend my time in fasting and praying for you."

Naturally the evangelists were very much hurt at Mr. Wang's refusal to eat. That evening again the meal was ready, and they earnestly pressed him to partake, but Mr. Wang continued fasting and praying for them. Next morning, almost distracted, the evangelists urged him to eat breakfast, but he refused again. By noontime all the stones of hindrance were removed out of the way, and Mr. Wang ate with them. When the devil gets in and divides God's children, is it not a precious boon when there is a man who can fast and pray till they are delivered.

For several years Mr. Wang was with me everywhere, and the very fact of such a scholar of note being with me, declaring his faith in the Son of God, made a mighty impression upon the people everywhere.

Once when several scholars from the gentry guild were calling on me I asked them:

"How does it come that you are putting off the acceptance of the Lord Jesus Christ as your Saviour so long? In the early years when there was so much uncertainty about us and the doctrines we preached there might have been some excuse for your delay. Now the proof in the transformed lives of so many ought to satisfy you. There is Mr. Wang Shih-ying, as great a scholar as any of you. He has not only accepted the Lord Jesus Christ as his Saviour, but for years has been preaching His Gospel."

"But," said they, "Mr. Wang Shih-ying was a good man before he ever became a Christian."

"Well, yes, that may be true, but is Mr. Wang a worse man since he became a Christian?"

"Oh no, he is much better."

"Then by your own admission Jesus Christ makes bad men good and good men better. What excuse can you offer for further delay?" One of them, touching his heart, said:

"There are more of us scholars who secretly believe than you imagine."

Mr. Wang has been, for years widely used not only in the Honan field, but in other parts of China. For many years he has been one of the most influential pastors in the Changte region.

3. A SCHOLAR SAVED FROM THE DEPTHS
(Hu Ting-Chang)

After I had used Wang Shih-ying several years as an evangelist the claim for a man of his scholarship for the Weihwei Normal School was so pressing that I yielded him up for that service,

I looked to the Lord to give me one as good to take his place. Some time before that a man, Hu Ting-Chang, equally as good a scholar as Wang Shih-ying, was converted at Peng-cheng, a large pottery center to the northwest of our field. He had led a very bad life. Once the man he had cruelly wronged caught him in the very act of sin. He became so enraged that he cut off one of Mr. Hu's fingers. Hu Ting-Chang, after conversion, gave abundant evidence that the Lord Jesus Christ had taken full control. He came on with me as a learner, and soon showed exceptional ability as a preacher. Wherever I went he accompanied me and was trained under fire, as all the most efficient workers have been.

When this man's reputation as a preacher and his character as a Christian were fully established, I was asked to give him up to another. Mr. Griffith was then in charge of the work in Changte city, where many scholars were constantly to be met with. He said it was impossible to carry on the work unless he was assisted by one of the ablest scholars we had. He appealed to me for Mr. Hu Ting-Chang. That service, it seemed to me, was the most important Mr. Hu could then render, and I gladly gave him to Mr. Griffith.

I have never met a man with a keener mind than Mr. Hu. He had the talents of an ecclesiastical lawyer, and was as true to us and the cause of Christ as any evangelist I have ever known. It is some years since he was called to a field of even wider service in China.

VIII. PROOFS OF GOD'S GRACE

From Nei Hwang County, Honan

I. A CHINESE SHAKESPEARE

IN THE autumn of 1890 we secured our first foothold in Honan. It was at the market town of Chu-wang. Our hope was that we might be located at the prefectural city of Changte, thirty miles farther west, but we found the opposition too strong. It was our intention, in taking Chu-wang, that it was simply a temporary place until we obtained a foothold in Changte.

After securing the compound, Dr. McClure and Mr. MacGillivary moved in with their belongings. They were not there more than two weeks before they were attacked by a mob which took away everything they possessed; they even attempted to carry off the kitchen stove, but it proved too heavy for them. They contented themselves, however, by taking away the stove lids. The persons of the missionaries were not harmed.

The case was taken to the British consul at Tientsin, and when the great Viceroy Li Hung-chang heard of it he sent orders that the things were to be restored or compensation made, and that we were to be allowed to carry on mission work from that center. These negotiations caused a delay of about a year in the work.

From Chu-wang we could reach a region with five or six million people. The sick flocked to the mission, so that Dr. McClure had in one year

81

twenty-eight thousand treatments. During that year he gave fifty-four people their sight by removing cataracts.

With a couple of Shantung preachers I visited all the villages round about this market town. The people were almost barbarous. The language was as bad as that of Sodom. We were repeatedly pelted with clods and brickbats, and hindered from speaking by the noise and constant raising of disturbances in the villages surrounding. We spent the winter of 1892-93 in that work.

One day in a certain village they were determined that we should not be able to speak at all. I first asked one of the Shantung evangelists to speak, but he could not get any hearing because of hooting and yelling. In despair he turned to me, and I asked another to take his place. That man fared no better. Then I undertook to speak, but also failed to get a hearing. Then I read the riot act to them in Matt. 10, and went on to explain it: "And whosoever shall not receive you, nor hear your words, when ye depart out of that house or city, shake off the dust of your feet. Verily I say unto you, It shall be more tolerable for the land of Sodom and Gomorrha in the day of judgment, than for that city" (Matt. 10:14, 15). Instantly an awe fell upon them. They ceased their opposition and begged us to go on preaching. They said, "We will listen" and when we were leaving they said, "Remember if ever you come again there will be no opposition."

Next day we came to the village of the Changs. There our reception was very cordial. Some well-dressed gentlemen brought out a table and chairs and asked us to be seated, offering us tea. These were Mr. Hu I-chwang and his brother Hu Feng-hwa. These men had been very wealthy. When their father died he left them a great estate, but through opium, gambling, and women they were quite poor. We preached there for a couple of hours, and continued our work in other villages.

By the year 1896 the Changs' village became so friendly that a Mr. Fan, a B.A. from that center came to teach Dr. Dow. Within a year he was a believer in the Lord Jesus Christ. In the spring of 1902 we recorded the Hu brothers and several other men. Mr. Fan, a relative of the teacher's, whom we examined along with them, appeared, from his sallow complexion, to be an opium-user. I asked him how long he had been using opium. He replied, "I have never used opium in my life." I had been so deceived in my judgment about him that I was ashamed now to ask any of the others if they were opium-users, so I passed over the Hu brothers. Later on they told me that they were in a tremble lest I put the question to them, and I found out that they were, up to that time, users of opium. They escaped, but they resolved that very day they would cease using the drug.

The elder Mr. Hu had written more than one hundred plays for Chinese theatricals. We called him "Shakespeare." He and his brother were notorious gamblers. They did not gamble for small stakes; they brought their well-to-do friends from several counties at a time, and they would have a regular bout of gambling. Theoretically gambling is against the laws of China. On one of these big occasions word came from the county town that the magistrate was going to seize them. They, however, defied the magistrate and prepared to defend themselves. The younger brother, Hu Feng-hwa was a great warrior. He could furnish a thousand men for the village fights.

At the time we recorded them as catechumens, I saw that the elder brother, Hu I-chwang, was a man of unusual promise and I invited him to come to Changte to stay with me for a year and study the Bible. I told him I could give no wages, but would provide his food. He readily consented and came.

Mr. Hu made remarkable progress in Bible study. After a couple of months I took him some church papers one day and said:

"Mr. Hu, I fancy you will get some good in reading these papers."

He replied: "You know I was forty-seven years of age before I ever got a chance to look into my [ord's Book, and still I know practically nothing about it. If you don't mind I would rather not spend time reading these church papers. I prefer to devote all my time to studying His Book.,,

Some people will spend more time on the daily newspapers than they will on the Word of God, and wonder why they do not grow in grace. Other people will spend more time on cards than they will on the Word of God; then they wonder why they do not grow in the knowledge of their Lord and Saviour Jesus Christ. Yet this man, just recently led out of heathenism, was so eager to study his Lord's Book that he had not time to read even church papers. His progress in the Word of God was certainly most encouraging to me. He memorized it wholesale. All the lists of sins in the Bible he could quote off as freely as if he were reading them.

After a year I sent him home to take on others for training. He hired a man to wheel a barrow with his bedding and books, and went around his county preaching Jesus. Soon there were scores of believers in Chang's village and surrounding country. Some years later the Hu brothers brought twenty other Christian leaders, both men and women, from their little church there to take part at the Hsunhsien fair. They came at their own expense.

About the close of the fair that year I said to Mr. Hu I-chwang:

"The students from the seven counties are coming up to Changte city for their examinations. There will be about four or five thousand of them, with their teachers and attendants, and they will be in the city a month. I wish you could come over and assist us during that wonderful time of opportunity."

Mr. Hu replied that he had already planned to be there. Later in this student work his help was most invaluable. Many of these Chinese students were "top heavy"—governors, sons, viceroys' sons or nephews, etc. They supposed that they knew everything worth knowing, but when they listened to a man like Mr. Hu with all the lore of China at his finger tips, they realized that here was a man who had forgotten more than they had ever learned. Besides that, he could testify to the Grace of God in Christ Jesus which had made a new man of him. Those were days of great opportunity in influencing the student body.

One day, when a change in the weather had come and it was blowing a cold northeastern wind, Mr. Hu came in without his overcoat. This I at once noticed, and said:

"Mr. Hu, where is your overcoat? When the weather is ordinary you come day after day wearing your overcoat, and now the weather suddenly turns cold and you come in without it. I am afraid you will get cold and be ill."

"Oh, don't mind about me. I am all right," he replied.

"But I must mind. I am afraid you will become ill and we will lose your help here with these students."

"No, no; don't mind about me. I am not cold," he continued to say.

"But I must mind," I said. "Where is your overcoat?" "Well," he said, "since you are bound to know, my food money ran out and I didn't want to lose this splendid opportunity with these young men, so I just pawned my overcoat that I might have money enough to keep me until the end of the month."

How many of us in Western lands have so much of the love of God in our hearts that we would pawn our overcoats in winter in order that we might get an opportunity to save our fellow men? I have listened to great preachers in different lands, but I have never listened to a greater preacher than Hu I-chwang. If we foreigners were ever inclined to get a little conceited about our knowledge of the Chinese language, we just had to listen to that torrent of phraseology and apt illustration that poured from this orator to be down in the dust once again. A certain mission offered him more than double the salary that he was getting with us, but, though extremely poor, he would not consider it and stayed on with us. He said all that he wanted was enough to live upon, that he might tell of his Saviour, Jesus. I don't remember ever hearing Mr. Hu speak of the Lord without prefixing the word, "Saviour" before the name. In his home chapel above the platform in large crimson and gold characters are the words— "Saviour Jesus."

Mr. Hu was a tireless worker. His whole soul seemed to go out in a desire to save his people. One incident in our great meetings in Changte was an example of this. Mr. Hu was standing pleading for sinners to come to their Saviour, pleading as only he could plead. Well-dressed students were going into the inquiry-room, when there came up to the front the most dilapidated-looking beggar. This beggar's father had once been the wealthiest man in Changte, but he had gone through all his estate and was now completely down and out. The beggar asked:

"Will the Lord receive me?"

Mr. Hu said: "Certainly He will receive you," and with beaming face he leaned down, took him by the hand, and led him up on to the platform. Sending him into the inquiry-room, Mr. Hu went on preaching.

Gifted preacher as he was, this man had the faith and humility of a little child. When he died the one testimony that was given by pastors, evangelists, and leaders at his grave was that no one ever saw him out of temper from the day he was converted until the day he died.

2. A FAITHFUL PASTOR
(Hu Feng-hwa)

Hu Feng-hwa, the younger brother of Hu I-chwang, was cast in an altogether different mold. His disposition was fierce and ungovernable. He was always a leader in any village fight, but the Grace of God changed him into the wonderful pastor that he became and continues to be until this day. He was called to be pastor over his hometown congregation at Changtsun. At the present time this church has a membership of about a thousand. There is a large school for boys, also a girls' school, both supported by themselves.

Once Hu I-chwang and his brother, along with other Christian leaders in that place, invited my wife and myself to hold a nine days' revival mission there. The audiences were so large we had to meet in the yard. One very peculiar thing about the meetings was that after I had finished the address and said to the audience, "You may pray and tell all about the things that hinder you," no one would pray. My custom is never to ask individuals to lead in prayer. I leave it all to the prompting of the Spirit of God. Here day by day for several days after each address, though I threw the meeting open for prayer, no one responded. After waiting for eight or ten minutes a hymn was sung. At the close of the hymn another opportunity was given for prayer, but they all were as silent as if a dumb devil had seized them.

Had I offended them? I had said to the people at the beginning of the meetings, that if they had any prayers they could rattle off without any heart meaning in them, they had better lay them on the shelf until after these meetings were over. There was no time for such timekilling prayers. That was all I had said. Surely there was no harm in telling them that. It seemed distressing that this should continue; however, I was confident of the final result, for on the fourth morning I had written in my diary:

"Up to the present there is no indication of revival. A dumb devil seems to have possession of the people, but as sure as God's Word is 'like fire and like a hammer that breaketh the rock in pieces' so surely shall these people bend to the dust before Him."

Just then the pastor, Mr. Hu, came in, greatly agitated. He said:

"We have started an extra prayer meeting; these services have been going on for three days and there is no indication of revival. If God does not revive us now, we might as well close up the church on Sunday. When the people hear that Dr. MacKenzie is going to be here on Sunday, the church is crammed; but ordinarily they won't come out at all."

After that our one difficulty was to get the meetings closed. When I gave the address on the fourth morning and threw the meeting open, they were breaking everywhere. One of the leaders and his son were at such enmity they were ready to kill each other. They were under the most intense conviction and confessed this in public. I thought the pastor's heart would burst, he was so broken. He went on to confess:

"I have kept urging the people to come to church on Sunday, but I allow my wife and daughters to go on doing all their sewing on Sunday. I have my hired man and my animals working in the fields on Sunday when the church service is going on. If I, the pastor, thus openly steal God's time, how can I expect to move the other people to obey Him?"

The meeting might be going on for three hours, and in despair I would pronounce the benediction, wanting them to scatter. Even then I have known people to rush up to the front and pour out all their hindering sins. Two noted witches living near by attended the meetings and were convicted of sin and saved. They begged the pastor and leaders to go home with them and take down all the gods and burn them. They had a bonfire of the gods, and prayed and drove the demons out. One young man said to me:

"I cannot account for the change that has come over the people of our village. Heretofore they would pay no heed to me when I would tell them of the Gospel, but today when I went home to my dinner almost a hundred of my fellow villagers gathered around, pleading with me to tell them about this wonderful Lord Jesus who was moving among us."

One man, who had formerly lived a very evil life, the year previously had professed faith in the Lord Jesus Christ and showed real transformation. Evidently the change had not been deep enough. He came forward one day, broken to the very depths. He said:

"I have been a hypocrite. My religion was only on the outside of me. For example, when the collection was to be given in on Sunday I would not give coppers or large cash, but I would feel around in my pocket to see if I could not pick out small cash, and to make believe that I was giving big ones I would cast them in with greater force to make them rattle. I just tremble now to think that God should have spared me with my half-hearted service. I was robbing God of his tithes."

The story of one man saved at these meetings deserves a space by itself.

3. SAVED FROM A FEED-BASKET
(Kwoa Lao-ts'wei)

SCRIPTURE TESTIMONY
Jesus is able to save to the uttermost
HEBREWS 7:25

There was a noted sinner, Kwoa Lao-ts'wei. At eighteen years of age his father died, leaving him a splendid farm and a fine prosperous business in one of the neighboring towns. This young Kwoa was then married to a young wife and had the brightest of prospects. As so many Chinese do, he gambled. Soon he became an addict to opium. His course downhill was rapid. He lost his business and his farm. His wife died of a broken heart and left one little daughter. But Kwoa at that time had another wife. No trouble to get another wife in China. She came in about as soon as the first wife was buried. She was a young creature, with no choice of her own. Her choice was made for her. When she realized the situation, with the husband absolutely gone with opium and nothing to live upon, she was crying her eyes out. The husband could not sleep at night unless he was dosed with opium. When he should have been in the prime of life he could not bear the weight of a coverlet over him. He might die off any moment, and she would be sold into a life of slavery and shame, for poor widows have no rights in China, and the little stepdaughter would be sold into the same kind of life.

When things had come to that crisis, these meetings were started at Changtsun, five miles away. One of the Changtsun Christians, Mr. Wu, a B.A., took a great interest in Mr. Kwoa because they were friends. He with several other Christians determined to bring Mr. Kwoa to the meetings to be saved. Mr. Kwoa, when he heard of their intention, made all manner of excuses, saying it was impossible for him to go. He said, "For one thing, I am so weak I could not think of trying to walk five miles." They replied: "We never expected you to. We have all come along to carry you there in a feed-basket." They removed all the excuses, and he got into the feed-basket, for he could not stand the jolts of a cart. Mr. Kwoa had gumption enough to see that when he got there he would not be able to get opium. He did not see how he was going to overcome the craving, so he manoeuvred to put away a lot of opium pills inside the lining of his garments. These Christian men, however knew the schemes of opium sots, and they felt over his garments and took out all the pills. Kwoa, in despair, said:

"What am I going to do when the craving comes on?"

"Don't mind that. We will pray for you, and you pray for yourself."

They brought Kwoa along, and had him at the meetings the first day. That evening, when it was time to retire, the craving was on most awfully. Kwoa said, "You have burned up all my pills, and now the craving is on. How can I ever pass this night?" Two of the Christians went on either side of him and marched him round and round the village until he was tired out. They then gave him a drink of tea and put him to bed. They knelt around and prayed with him. Kwoa said he was more than amazed when he awoke and found it was daylight next morning. He had not had such a sleep for years. The following night the craving was on again as bad as ever. They marched him around the village as before, got him thoroughly tired out, prayed for him, and he slept through the next night all right. When the meetings were ended Kwoa went home a saved man.

In a few years Kwoa was one of the most eloquent preachers we had. He was next to Hu I-chwang in eloquent power. For years he went with me as one of my preachers. Once my wife and I spent several days with the preaching band at Mr. Kwoa's village. He would stand up before the crowd from his own and neighboring villages, and say:

"Friends, you know what I had become at forty-five years of age. You know that through opium and gambling I was regarded as the lowest. I had no property; I could not sleep a wink unless I was dosed with opium. At that time there was no hope for me, no hope for my wife and child. You all know that. And then the Lord Jesus came, reached down, and took me right out of the horrible pit and the miry clay. He put my feet upon the rock and established my goings. Before the change, I could not walk two miles to save my life; I was too weak. Now I am sixty years of age and I can walk in to Changte, thirty miles, without noticing it. I have my property back; I am as well off as I ever was; I have a wife and four happy children. My eldest daughter is a graduate of the girls' school in Changte, my second daughter is in her second year in higher- primary school, and I have a son and daughter in the lower primary at Changte. They are all believers and followers of the Lord Jesus Christ. Surely if any man has the right to commend the Lord Jesus to sinners, I have that right, because I have proven that he is able to save to the uttermost."

These three men whom I have mentioned as leaders, the Hu brothers and Mr. Kwoa, are all monuments of divine grace; all were called to reap in His plenteous harvest field, and with notable success. Once when a county magistrate came to take over the seals of office at the Neihwang county town, the following day, as many good magistrates do, he dressed himself in the garb of an ordinary scholar and went secretly on a tour of inspection through his county. The county has always been notorious for the number of its robbers and bad characters. He arrived at Changtsun village one hot afternoon. He said to a man in the village:

"Would you mind giving me a drink? A cup of cold water will do."

The man whom he asked was a Christian. He said: "Your Honor, come into the school and drink tea."

"What? You know me?" the magistrate asked, in surprise.

"Yes," he said. "I happened to be in the county town last night when you came in to take over your seals."

Said the magistrate: "I have come on purpose to Changtsun to look into the church here." So he saw the fine church building and asked: "Did the foreigners build this? How much money did they put into it?"

"Nothing. We built it ourselves." They took him to the boys' school with one hundred and twenty-five boys and several teachers. "Is this supported with foreign money?" he asked.

"Why, no, not a dollar of foreign money goes into this. We pay for this ourselves."

The magistrate said : "I would that all the people in my county were Christians just like you people are here belonging to this church. If all the people of my county were Christians as you are, I would not need to spend any money on police support."

Some people say they do not believe in foreign missions. What grander results from the expenditure of money than what we see in this Christian movement in Neihwang County?

After the great revival movement in Changte in 1908 Dr. MacKenzie with the revival leaders went to Changtsun for a few days. As many as five thousand people assembled. Again at Christmas time the Christians could hardly keep up with and teach the numbers of heathen that were coming there inquiring.

After the famine was over we went there with the preaching band, and were there for several days. One day while I was speaking to fully eleven hundred people in the tent they told me that even more were outside, being spoken to by Chinese leaders. During that time there were one hundred and six professed converts or inquirers. These were at once put on the course for catechumens, and months later the pastor, Mr. Hu, said that they accepted one hundred and two out of that number as catechumens.

IX. HOW WE REACHED THE STUDENTS

"All things to all men."
(Mr. Niu)[1]

M R. NIU was a village school-teacher in the hills west of Changte. We first met him when he came up for the B.A. examinations in 1898. At that time he was in the city about a month, with thousands of other students from the seven counties.

During the examinations a year earlier we had used only the straight preaching of the Gospel. Sometimes we had fair order, but at other times not. Students the world over are not renowned for keeping good order, and Chinese students are no exception to the rule. We must remember that some of these students were from noted families, and it might not dawn on them that they could learn something even from a foreigner. At times when we tried to keep order the whole roomful would bolt amid rowdy laughter.

In 1898 we were prepared with globes, maps, and astronomical charts in our study. While constant proclamation of the Gospel went on in the chapel at the front of the compound, I would say to the students, "We can accommodate about thirty of you in our study at a time. When we give a short talk with that many and show them around the house, we will let them out at the back gate and come for another thirty" This plan

---

1   Pronounced New.

pleased everybody and a large number were always hearing the Gospel. If they would not behave themselves and listen, there was no hope that they could get back to see the house.

We have taken eighteen hundred and thirty-five men through our house in a single day, and the same day my wife received hundreds of women. The preaching was going on continually at the front, but at intervals a crowd of a couple of hundred men were brought in, and I would preach to them for a while from the veranda. When taking them through the house we had to have Christians at every turn lest all portable articles disappear in the students capacious sleeves. They were all led through the study and dining-room and kitchen, and above all the cellar, and were then let out by the back gate, while a fresh crowd came in from the *front*.

We made a special point, when a band of students was down in the cellar with us, to lift every lid off box and jar and have them look in. That completely did away with the absurd stories that we bought up little children, then, after taking out their eyes and hearts to make quinine and other effective medicines, we salted the flesh down in jars to eat. These young scholars had seen all with their own eyes and were ever ready to testify to the falsity of these reports.

When the students came we always gave them special attention because of their influence throughout the country. The first thing in my study which caught the students' eyes was the large globe, and they would want it explained. At first none could accept the fact that the world turned round! "Wouldn't we all fall off if it did?" was a question constantly heard. When it was explained how the Creator had arranged the laws of attraction so that it was impossible to fall off, then many would believe. Some, however, were found always ready to dispute. They would contend that the earth was flat and that the sun rose and set. For proof they would say, "We know that the sun at night goes down into the western sea and during the night it passes through the water under the earth and consequently is all cooled off in the morning." We met this by showing the sun's distance from the earth and of the utter impossibility that the sun would sweep round its enormous circle every twenty-four hours, but how easy for our earth, like a wheel on its hub, to face round to the sun in that time. Instantly they sought explanation.

By the time we got away up among the fixed stars— those enormous bodies—their uncountable distances, and their unthinkable velocity whirling through space, the pride and self-conceit oozed out of them. It was time then to ask, "Which one of your temple gods has been able to create and control this amazing universe of ours?" Here and there you would hear one exclaim, "Truly we are like frogs down in a well looking up at the heavens and imagining that we see the whole expanse." At that stage it was possible to tell of Him Who is Lord over all and Who upholds all these by the word of His power.

One day when the students were coming by the hundreds to see us, the magistrate's brother, with a couple of secretaries, spent the whole afternoon with us and heard what we said to the different bands. Just at sundown, when they were leaving, the brother of the magistrate said:

"We have been very uneasy owing to the great number of students coming out here. My brother sent us out today to see how you managed so many without riot. If these students became ugly, we have not sufficient force of police to quell them. On the street today as we came here we were constantly meeting students returning, who were telling their fellows going out, 'The foreigners will heartily receive you, talk to you, and show you everything.' When I report to my brother, the magistrate, how you manage he will not be anxious, for your method with the students is more effective in keeping order than a force of hundreds of soldiers."

The most I have done in a single day was to talk to fourteen different bands of students and then in the evening to go into the city and preach to them in the street chapel. That day, however, it was impossible to eat a regular meal. I was kept going by taking a cup of hot milk at intervals.

It was that night in the street chapel that Mr. Niu came under conviction and believed in the Lord Jesus Christ. When the exams were over, Mr. Niu went home and told his wife of his new-found faith. Mrs. Niu was a strong-minded woman and flew into a rage and reviled her husband high and low, vowing she would never become one of the detestable "number two devils." Next day she went to her mother's home, where fuel was added to the fire. It was agreed that such disgrace could not and would not be endured. On returning home she reviled her husband with redoubled vigor. She was puzzled over her husband's attitude, for never before did she attempt to revile him without getting the worst of it. Now he made no attempt at reply, and did not get angry, either. She ended the bout by taunting him with the fact that through eating the Jesus doctrine he had lost his manhood and couldn't talk back to a woman. Next day her fury had not abated and she screamed at him:

"I won't cook or sew for you, so you may starve and go in rags." Beside herself with rage, she spat in his face, and from past experience expected surely a knock-down blow; but he did not lift a hand and, wiping the spittle off, went over into a corner of the yard and prayed. That day he took his meal at the eating-house on the street, and the wife was chagrined that she could not starve him into submission.

On the following day her rage knew no bounds and she followed up her reviling with a blow in her husband's face. Judging from all past experience, she fully expected her husband would almost kill her, but to her utter amazement he did nothing. All that day he fasted and prayed, and in telling this story she said: "That evening it came over me that I was the wickedest woman on earth and that I was the crazy one, and not my husband!" The glow on her face as she told me how the Lord Jesus triumphed from that hour was good to behold. Mr. Niu for many years has been one of our most beloved and successful pastors and his wife has all through the years been a zealous and honored helpmate to her husband.

In this chapter we have made mention of the reception of Chinese in our home. When we went to open the important prefectural city of Changte my wife and I agreed, no matter how much extra trouble was entailed, we would keep open house that we might win some. Even if a beggar came in a teachable mood, he found a welcome. For years I tried to get in contact with a noted scholar in the city, but he seemed unapproachable. His younger brother believed, and so did the teacher in their private school, yet this man seemed to avoid me. Imagine, then, my delight when one day it was announced that he was at the front, waiting to see me. I hastened out to meet him and, grasping both his hands in mine, I told him how delighted I was to see him. His first words were:

"You have a fine reputation among us scholars because you receive the lowliest and poorest among our people with the same heartiness as the highest and the wealthiest. We scholars all approve of that spirit, but our shame is that we too seldom practice it." With such an opening it was easy to tell of the lowly Jesus.

I had always left strict orders with the gate-keeper that when anyone asked to see me with the avowed purpose of learning this doctrine of salvation, he must bring that request in to me for my decision. On no account must he decide it. But gate-keepers in China have a streak of laziness and indifference in their make-up, as perhaps in other lands. Repeatedly scholars and other men of importance, when I was visiting them in their home places, said that they had repeatedly called to see me, and had been refused admittance. One day I happened just to arrive at the big gate when two scholar friends approached. I delightedly received them, saying, "I expected you to call on me long ere this."

They replied, "We have repeatedly come to your gate, but have been refused admittance." I took advantage of this to warn the gate-keeper before them that it was not for him to decide who should see me or who should not, and hinted that his position would depend upon obedience.

In the early years of our trying to get a foothold in Changte we were opposed by a very noted scholar. He along with others carried the opposition so far that I had to take it to the British ambassador, and these

> **SCRIPTURE TESTIMONY**
>
> *The heart of the believer, like Jesus, is full of compassion*
>
> MATTHEW 9:36-38 · GALATIANS 6:2 · EPHESIANS 4:32 · COLOSSIANS 3:12

opponents were made to offer an apology. Years passed, and the father of this noted scholar was so ill that he came to Dr. Menzies for treatment. At the time his son was an acting official in Peking. On coming home to see his father it would be contrary to Chinese etiquette if he did not call at the mission to give thanks for what had been done. When he arrived at my study he had the usual lofty air of a Chinese scholar. I did not mind it, for I knew that my opportunity would soon come.

As we sat chatting he noticed the globe, and inquired as to its use. This explained, I asked him if he cared to have me explain the astronomical charts that were on the wall. He assured me he would be delighted. Step by step we went away up until we were talking on the fixed stars, their distances, their magnitude, their velocity. Finally he said, "Stop! Stop! You have taken me beyond my depth."

It was easy then to talk about the Creator of all things. He appeared as humble as a child as he went on listening to what I believed about the one Living and True God and about His Son from Heaven. During our conversation he had repeatedly spoken about a missionary friend in Peking with whom he was acquainted. I was well aware that that missionary had largely departed from the faith and was devoting his time to social service ideas, hoping to gain the friendship of Chinese men of note in that way. I asked if that man did not explain about the one Living and True God.

"No," he said, "he did not."

"What then," I asked, "could be the subject of his conversations?"

He said it was along the line of all the wonderful Western progress and inventions of every sort, such as bridges, steamboats, etc. By the time he was ready to depart he seemed to believe all that I had told him about God and about Jesus Christ and the way of salvation. In parting he said: "Remember, we are friends; we are not to stand on ceremony with each other. If I call on you, you are to receive me just as you are, and if you call on me it will be the same."

A few days later he called again. At once he said, "I have been very much puzzled since our last conversation. I have been trying to find out the underlying motive of this foreign-mission effort in China. For example, you know that you are not invited to our country. On the other hand, you are opposed at every step. Wherever you go you are reviled and taunted. Moreover, at times you are in danger of physical violence from rowdy crowds. Yet on and on you go proclaiming this Gospel. You are getting results, for men once notoriously vile are living decent, respectable lives. What is the motive that makes you come? Evidently it is not because you couldn't make a living in your own country. Take for example your doctors. Without a doubt they are well-educated people. They come to our country, and at great expense open up hospitals and treat endless streams of patients. What amazes us is that these doctors with their fingers will open up and cleanse out foul sores. Dear me, we scholars couldn't be induced to go near some of these offensive creatures. Yet your doctors seem delighted to do it, and that without pay. But perhaps to us scholars the most surprising of all is that you open schools for our poor children. Most of our Chinese people are too poor to send their children to school. We scholars and well-to-do people, of course, all have our private teachers, but it never occurs to us to invite our poor neighbor to send along his children to take advantage of our teacher. I have a poor neighbor who has four or five boys; they can never possibly get a schooling. I haven't felt the slightest urge to have him send his boys to study along with mine. But you foreigners come here to our country and you open up schools everywhere, and teach our children free of charge. What can be the underlying motive?

Then I took him through the Scriptures, first taking up the verse, "The love of Christ constraineth us; because we thus judge, that if one died for all, then were all dead; and that he died for all, that they which live should not henceforth live unto themselves, but unto him which died for them, and rose again (II. Cor. 5:14-15). Our whole theme during the conversation concentrated around the love of Christ, and his face lit up, and he said: "I understand it now. When you love Him and obey Him, you must come to our country no matter what the consequences would be." So far as I could see, he seemed to accept the fact of our Saviour and His great salvation. In a few days he returned to Peking and in a short time he died. I fain would hope that this noted scholar really believed in the Lord Jesus Christ and that I shall meet him in heaven.

People have come from the most distant places in the seven counties of our prefecture, saying, "We have been told that you freely receive people and talk the doctrine to them and show them around your home." We can best illustrate the influence which has gone out everywhere from this method of being all things to all men by telling what we met with on one short tour.

It was time for me to tour through the west and northwest of my field. Mr. Lochead, who had enough language to make his first tour profitable, came along. After walking forty *li* we were heartily received in the home of the wealthiest man in our large county. The young men of the family had been received by us when up for examinations, and the head of that home naturally appreciated our kindness. Going west a few *li* farther, we came to Shuiyeh, a town of thirty thousand, where all the Christians of that district had assembled to meet us. Presently several of the leading gentry of the town came and pressed us to visit with them, for, said they, "You were so kind to our boys when up at the examinations." Next day we came to Mr. Niu's village in the hills. By that time he and his wife had so lived Christ in their small market town that we met with a very friendly reception.

The following day we traveled about fifty *li* and arrived at a large market town close under the high mountains. Evidently the people there had never seen a foreigner, for they seemed a little frightened. The crowd stood about twenty feet away. When speaking I wanted closer contact, and as I went nearer they shied off. This was distressing, for it lasted about half an hour. Just then some well-dressed men came up and invited us to visit in their home. "Our boys," explained they, "were kindly received by you when they were in the city attending examinations, and it is only fitting that we return the compliment." It turned out that they were the most noted family in Lin County, and one of its members, a Hanlin scholar, was in a high place in Peking. The common people were afraid of us no longer and crowded round while we preached till midnight.

Going on from there on the fourth day, we had the mishap of a mule stumbling while fording a river and getting some of our bedding soaked. That day a man and his son repairing a fence by the roadside greeted us most kindly. We inquired if they had ever visited us at Changte, and the farmer said, "No," but that one of his sons while up at the examinations had been spoken to by us and shown all over our house. About four o'clock that afternoon it came on a steady downpour. Now the bedding on all the mulebacks was in for a soaking. Darkness came on and still we were far from the inn we must stop at. The soaked bundles on the mules became heavier and they fell behind. Still it poured and we plodded on through the deep-mud in the center of the road, for there was a ditch on either side.

About six-thirty we reached the inn, but gave up all hope of the animals with our baggage reaching it that night. The innkeeper was most unusual in his kind attention for our comfort in such a plight. He kindled a fire to dry our soaked garments, and soon had a fine supper ready for us. The animals with our things did finally turn up. The innkeeper in the morning was just as full of kindness as ever. I remarked to Mr. Lochead that this was most unusual attention on the part of an innkeeper and that our bill was likely to be large in proportion. When I asked for our bill he said:

"You don't owe me anything."

"What!" I said. "You can't run an inn for nothing."

His eyes filled with tears and he said: "My son, who is dead now, when up for examinations was kindly received in your home. Surely for his sake I can only treat you as a friend."

Going on, we arrived at the city of Shehsien, two hundred and forty li northwest of Changte. In a short time we were visited in our inn by the school inspector for the county, and one of the influential city school-teachers who had been received by us, along with their students, when attending the examinations at Changte.

Thus we might continue telling how doors were opened and access given for the Gospel throughout seven counties and among three millions of people by resolving that we would be all things to all men.

X. NOTHING TOO HARD FOR OUR GOD

AMONG THE BANDITS

A FTER DEVOTING about five years to missions for the deepening of spiritual life of Christians in many provinces, it seemed best that we should have a portion of our old field to work between times. The mission assigned us a portion containing seven or eight hundred towns and villages. In mid-harvest we started for Sun-tao, a small market town thirty-five li to the northeast, to commence work. As we were about to leave and on our carts, Dr. Leslie in saying good-by remarked:

"I guess you will have rather an idle time of it, this busy season of the year. The people will be too busy to pay any heed to what you have to say."

"Very well," I replied, "we will devote that time to the study of the Bible, getting better prepared for the people when they are ready to listen."

We secured control of two compounds for the work. The one on the north side, where we lived, was for women's work, which was carried on by my wife and her Bible women. There was a grocery store at the front, and we had to pass through this to the courts beyond. From the first day the yard was crowded with women and girls.

On the south side of the street a little farther east we rented a compound for men's work. The storekeeper, our landlord, was an opium-user. His eldest son and the one clerk that they used were also opium sots and much given to gambling and other vices. This eldest son was furious at his father for renting the place to the foreigners. Right opposite the place for men's work was a big gambling-den. They hindered us very much by the noise and commotion that went on there. Sometimes in the daytime we had crowds, but every night our place was crammed, and men standing away out onto the street.

In fifteen days the gambling-den had to close up because they had no customers, for they all came over to us, among them being the storekeeper's eldest son who had hated us so thoroughly. The man who was the Christian leader there, at that time, was an ex-bandit. His life had been notorious as a sinner. Shortly after he became somewhat interested in this new faith he attended the great revival at Changte in November, 1908. There, according to his own testimony, he was overawed at the mighty judgments of God, and was made a new man in Christ Jesus.

SCRIPTURE TESTIMONY
God answers prayer
LUKE 18:7 · JOHN 15:7 · ACTS 12:5 · JAMES 5:15

This Sun-tao region had perhaps more bandits to the square mile than any other part of China. It was almost impossible to pass through the region without molestation. All that we had to do, day by day, to show the handiwork of the Lord Jesus Christ, was to let the people see the change in this ex-bandit. Soon converts began to multiply, so much so that we had to rent extra places in order to accommodate the inquirers.

Formerly in the early years I always used to have about ten or twelve evangelists and probationary evangelists accompanying me on preaching tours. Now these were being used by the other missionaries who had taken over my field during my absence. Therefore, when we started out on this fresh work they could only allow me one of my old evangelists. It was Mr. Tung, and he was a good one. His life was absolutely consecrated to the Lord Jesus Christ; he was a powerful speaker and had a winning personality. Besides Mr. Tung there was just a young stripling, a learner, the son of one of our old evangelists. My wife had only her one Bible woman to assist her, and the work went on often up till about midnight.

After twenty days of this heavy strain we were all about broken down. So deeply was I impressed by our need for more workers that I went to my knees in a very agony of intercession to the Lord of the harvest to send us more laborers. While I was praying the answer came. So convinced was I that the answer *had* come that I went right to my wife and said: "Be at rest. The Lord is going to send us extra workers."

Next day Chang-Ching, our splendid elder of the Linchang church, who was in business in that city, came and said to us:

"I feel that I dare not continue in business any longer while souls are dying all about us. Could you make use of me to preach the Gospel?"

I said: "Of course we can. It was just yesterday that God said He was going to send workers, and you are the first to come."

He has been working as an Evangelist ever since.

A few days later two B.A.'s, government-school teachers, who had been converted a few years previously, came to me and said:

"Other men can teach these government-school students as well as we, but since souls are dying all around us, while the harvest is plenteous and laborers are few, we violate conscience by going on teaching school. Can you make use of us preaching?" We took them on, and they have been preaching ever since.

A short time after, Kwoa Lao-T'swei, a converted opium sot, came from the east, saying:

"I feel I must preach the Gospel. Can you make use of me?"

Within that year we had more than a dozen men and women whom the Lord had sent us.

On coming to China I felt deeply convinced that God was more concerned about the reaping of His harvest fields than I could possibly be. Therefore I always kept praying that the Lord of the harvest would send forth suitable harvesters into His field. I was always on the lookout for such men. I never waited until I saw perfection in them before I tested them out. It was plain to me that we foreigners were not perfect, and I could not expect that quality from men just up from heathenism, with all its debasing environment.

As I look back over the years of service in Honan I can count up about fifty men who have become evangelists and pastors, all of whom were induced to enter the service of the Kingdom (by the Grace of God) through me. I say this not for self-glorification, but to impress, upon young missionaries especially, the fact that *definite faith in God and obedience will certainly bring results.*

More than half of these had been sinners as vile as the devil could make them. But our almighty Saviour the Lord Jesus reached down and took them out of the horrible pit and the miry clay and placed their feet upon the Rock and established their goings, and put a new song into their mouths, even praise unto our God. The heathen did not require a microscope to tell that these men had passed from death unto life, from the power of Satan to be under the control of the Living God.

I was once asked by a missionary in another mission how it came to be that the Lord was using us to convert such notorious sinners. Said he:

"My Chinese pastor and myself have often discussed this, and we wonder how it comes about. So it was agreed that I should ask you the secret."

I replied: "The only secret is to preach the Gospel of the Lord Jesus Christ. I preach that God sent His own blessed Son to be sin for them that they might be made the righteousness of God in Him, and the love of Christ constrains them since they know that He died for them and rose again, and they live forever in the newness of life. It is not by might, nor by power, but by the Spirit of God."

SCRIPTURE TESTIMONY
Demons cast out in Jesus' name
MATTHEW 8:16-17 · MATTHEW 8:28-32 · MATTHEW 9:32-34 · MARK 1:23-26 · MARK 9:20-27 · LUKE 10:17

Just a few miles east of this market town of Sun-tao where we were working there lived a man named Ch'en Lao-Jung. He was one of the most noted men of the whole region. He, among other attainments, acted as a witch doctor, in control of evil spirits. Many people afflicted by demons would have him come and by his incantations cast out the evil spirit. But finally an evil spirit that he could not dislodge took possession of his old mother. He tried every device, but in vain. He loved his mother, and would have sacrificed his life to deliver and save her. So he settled down in despair. Just then a Christian relation of his, in passing his home, dropped in, and Mr. Ch'en asked him:

"Can your God cast out demons?"

"Of course He can."

"But can He cast out big demons? I can cast out small demons, but I cannot cast out this big demon that has taken possession of my mother."

The Christian answered: "The Saviour who saved us is the Lord Jesus Christ, the Son of God. He has all power in heaven and on earth. Big demons and little demons are all the same to Him. He has no trouble in casting them out."

"Then won't you pray for my mother and ask the Lord Jesus Christ to come and cast the demon out of her?"

"Of course I will." And forthwith he prayed, and the demon was cast out.

The old lady, when delivered, said: "Oh, you have come! How are you? Won't you drink tea?" Her son rejoiced greatly at seeing this deliverance. The Christian stayed there overnight and there was great peace and joy in the home. Next morning he had no sooner left than the demon returned and took possession again. A couple of days later the Christian returned to see how the Ch'en family was getting along. Mr. Ch'en said:

"Your Jesus works while you are here, but as soon as you go the demon comes back and takes possession."

"It is little wonder" said the other. "Look at all these gods around your house. Jesus sees that this home doesn't belong to Him. You will have to get all these gods removed."

"What?" said Ch'en. "Is it just these incense pots and these gods that stand between my mother and deliverance from the demons?"

"Yes," said his Christian friend. "You get rid of all these proofs of devil worship, and you and your whole house decide to serve the Living God, and the demon will not have any chance to come back here where the Lord reigns."

"Agreed," said Mr. Ch'en. "You help me and we will take them all down."

They tore all the gods down and smashed the incense pots and threw them out. Again they prayed, and the demon was cast out, and the old mother to the end of her days lived in the happy consciousness that Jesus Christ dwelt in her heart by faith.

In due time the storekeeper whom we have already mentioned, and his eldest son, the noted gambler and opium sot, and the clerk in the store, all became true converts to the Lord. When the eldest son realized that he had been delivered by the power of God, he went home to tell his mother. As soon as her son had announced that he had become a follower of the Lord Jesus Christ, she flew into a rage, and said:

"Kneel down." She spat in his face and boxed his ears and said: "I would rather see you dead than become a follower of those foreign devils."

"But, Mother," answered the son, "you know what a vile wretch I had become. Father could do nothing with me. The devil completely controlled my life. Do you want me to go on with harlots and opium and gambling, and squander the remaining few acres we own?"

The mother in a fury said: "Yes, I am willing that you should live as you have lived, and squander the last acre we own, but I cannot stand the disgrace of your linking up with these foreign devils. I will starve you." And after that for weeks and months he got slim fare.

In the meantime his wife and younger brother, with his wife, all had become believers. One evening when they were all learning hymns in the home there was a terrible hubbub outside. The mother in alarm cried:

"What's that? What's up?"

Her son replied: "Mother, the soldiers have come and raided that gambling-den just down the street, and they are taking off the gamblers to prison. But for the Lord Jesus Christ your son would be among them."

"Oh," said the old woman, "I will be a Christian, too. I will go that way, too. We will all go." And from that time on she became an earnest follower of her Saviour. Young Mr. Ch'en and their clerk became effective evangelists. The former went in triumph to be with the Lord some years later. Their clerk is still preaching and is one of our most faithful of evangelists.

The following year we arranged for some weeks of work in a market town across the river northeast from Sun-tao. Before we left Changte we were told that the bandits had complete possession of that center. Since, however, we had planned for that time and the accommodation was already arranged for, my wife and I went there with our workers.

The people throughout the region were afraid to come to the market lest they be robbed coming or going or at the market. Consequently, our audiences were mainly bandits. We have seen these bandits in tears. They would come to us, and say:

"Oh, if we could only pull out of this! But we have given our word of honor that we will stand together with the robber band and we will be shot if we pull out."

This band of more than two hundred men had a feud with another band of about equal size just south of the river. The day after one of these bandits decided to believe in the Lord Jesus Christ as his Saviour there was a fight, and he was shot.

Since we could not get the people of the surrounding country to come in to hear the Gospel, we decided, after two weeks, to leave the place and go back to Sun-tao. When we left in the early morning there were more than twenty bandits out to see us off. Among those bidding us farewell was the son of the chief.

Later while working at Sun-tao, one evening about ten o'clock it was announced that the bandits had carried off one of our chief Christians from a village a short distance north of the town. My two preachers at that time were ex-bandits. I said to them:

"Take my foreign lantern and go to the bandit center where they have carried this Christian, and say to them from me that up to the present we have not interfered with their work and they have not interfered with ours, therefore we have been on friendly terms, but now, since they begin to carry off our Christians, we cannot stand for it, and we will have to carry the matter to the official. If they will let this Christian come home in the morning we will not give word to the official." These two men took my lantern, located the man, and gave the bandits my message. One young bandit spoke up: "If all people became Christians, then what would we bandits have to live on?" That young rascal had twice gone with the bandits and carried off his own father for ransom. But these evangelists were firm and gave him my message, and after consultation they let the Christian man come back with them.

Next morning at breakfast-time one of the chief men among the bandits came to me and apologized. He said, "We will not take any more of your people off." A few days later our whole band, male and female workers, went right into the bandit center. We took up our position a few rods from the headquarters of the bandits. While speaking we would have bandits sitting all around with their rifles slung over their shoulders. Loot and stolen things were being constantly brought in—ows, donkeys, mules, etc. I managed to make it so hot for the bandits who had rifles over their shoulders that in very shame they carried them off and put them into the headquarters office.

While speaking I noticed one young bandit becoming very much agitated. I supposed he had suddenly turned ill. On finishing, I asked one of my ex-bandit preachers to speak. He was not speaking long before he sized up the situation with the young bandit. He saw he was under conviction. He let another ex-bandit go on with the preaching and, taking this young fellow by the hand, led him away to a quiet place to talk with him. This young bandit happened to be the same young fellow who had said, "If all people became Christians, then what would we bandits have to live on?" and who had twice gone with the others to take his own father away for ransom. He decided to become a Christian and give up banditry, and the exbandit preacher went with the young fellow to interview the bandit leader, who gave him permission to go. When he handed in his rifle the bandit leader said: "Just wait a moment. There is your share of loot coming to you."

The young fellow said: "No, I want nothing." And he came home with us that night.

Among those converted at this Sun-tao center was a fine young man who was working part of the farm of one of the wealthy landowners. The friends of this landowner were making mock of him because he allowed this Christian to work his land. He told his son to approach the young farmer, saying:

"I have no objection to your being a Christian if you will only work at it quietly. I don't want you to go to church on Sunday. You can be a Christian and leave those things out. I don't want you to be singing your hymns around my farm. Then if you agree to that," said the son, "my father will be able to meet the jeers of his friends and allow you to work the farm."

"No," said the young Christian, "I cannot do that. We Christians are the only Bible the unsaved are reading."

So the landowner turned him off the land and had others come to work it. Within a year he was thoroughly sick of those gambling, drinking fellows, and told his son to go and get that Christian back to work the farm.

On one of our visits to Sun-tao we were met about halfway by fourteen well-mounted, fully armed soldiers. They greeted us very cordially and insisted on acting as our escort the rest of the way, where they showed us every honor, to the wonder and amazement of the village folk. For days soldiers kept coming from the camp to our meetings and many showed a real desire to learn the way of salvation. We found these men so friendly that I began to wonder if there was not some cause for this most unusual attitude on the part of Chinese soldiers.

Then one day the captain of the band called upon me and told the following story. He had in his camp for some time just one Christian soldier, who lived such a consistent Christian life as to win the respect and esteem of both officers and men. All the captain could tell of him was that he had come from a Christian family about one hundred and fifty miles south of the Yellow River. "Ten days ago," the captain said, "just before you came, I was out one night with a band of my men after certain robbers whom we knew to be in a village near by. I suspected the robbers to be around a certain corner, but was not sure. I was about to step forward to scout when the Christian held me back, saying, 'Your life is more valuable than mine. Let me go.' He went forward with rifle ready. The next instant he had shot and killed the robber chief, who with his band were hiding around the corner, but before he could step back he fell with a shot through the head." As this heathen captain closed the story the tears ran down his cheeks and he added, "Yes, he died for me, his captain."

Before the captain left he had arranged with me to conduct public Christian funeral services for the dead man. At this service all the Christians of the region were present and an impressive funeral procession was arranged when soldiers and Christians marched through the village to do honor to the brave Christian who had given his life for his captain.

The year after the great famine my wife and I with a band of male and female workers went throughout the Changte field. These meetings were conducted from place to place, lasting five months, and more than three thousand men and women gave in their names as inquirers.

XI. THE STORY OF MR SU, MY TRUSTED

CO-WORKER

IN 1914, one of our young missionaries had just finished his language course and was appointed to take charge of the work in the city of Changte. He came to me and said:

"Here they have appointed me to oversee the work in this big city, and I don't know how to begin. Won't you give me a start?"

I replied: "I would be delighted to help you, but in order to do anything in this city now you will have to do something extraordinary."

He asked: "What do you mean by 'having to do something extraordinary'?"

I said: "Simply this, that the street chapel has been allowed to run down and something unusual must be done."

"Well," he continued, "what do you propose?"

"I propose getting a suitable site as near the center of the city as possible, and I would put up a big mat pavilion seating at least seven hundred people, and I would go on with meetings morning, noon, and night for at least half a month." The young missionary thought this was capital, and hastened to interview the other missionaries about it. At once they commenced to pour cold water upon the scheme, saying: "Goforth must be a fool. If he cannot get people into the chapel already rented, why go to the expense of putting up a big mat shed? At any rate, as far as we are concerned, there is no Canadian money for that scheme."

The young man came back to me all in the blues, saying, "The thing won't go."

I replied: "It shall go, for a lady down in Australia has just sent me a gift of fifty pounds to do what I like with, and I choose to put some of that money into the building of this mat pavilion; so go ahead. I now have several weeks of special meetings over in Shansi. By the time I return I want you to have that pavilion up, and we will begin."

On my return home the pavilion was all ready. After a day's rest we commenced. Forenoon and afternoon we had special meetings for the Christians. Between meetings and all evening were devoted to direct evangelistic preaching to the heathen. After a few days the Spirit of God was moving mightily among the Christians. At times it was like judgment among them, and many were confessing their sins in brokenness and tears.

Among others moved was one of our pastors. At the time of the Boxer movement he was misled by a certain scholar, who induced him to use the church's influence to open a coal mine without official sanction. This scholar had always been a thorn in our side because of his wonderful influence over the evangelists and pastors. He was so slippery it was hard to catch him. He so managed lawsuits that he kept the magistrate in hot water. We forbade him coming into the mission compound at all because of his evil influence among the Christian leaders. This did not hinder him, because he got into contact with them in the city.

The first symptom of this pastor's being led the wrong way was his commencing to put on finer clothes. He was brought up before a committee of the foreign missionaries, but denied it all, and since the case was in doubt he was allowed off. One day in these special meetings he was mightily moved, and he stripped off his fine coat and threw it on the platform. He said, "I have gotten this by wrong means and I cannot wear it any more." While he did this he was so broken up he could hardly get his ideas out. The scholar who had led him astray was in the audience that day. The Spirit of God brought him under mighty conviction. He broke down and confessed with loud cries his sins. The conversion of this scholar seemed so wonderful to all that it was not long before he was used as one of the regular evangelists. Though previously I had had to be severe with him because of his evil influence over others, from the moment of his conversion I believe he would have died for me any day. This man, after some years of preaching, perished in a flooded river that he was bound to cross to keep an appointment.

After the Lord commenced to work mightily among the Christians, the unsaved in the audience came under conviction. The tent prepared to seat seven hundred, instead of being too large was too small. Sometimes as many as a thousand or more were there seeking entrance. We had to roll up the sides of the tent to give them hearing. After fifteen days one of the missionaries said, "This is one of the greatest surprises we have ever met with. It will never do to stop these meetings now. You must go on." I fortunately had some spare time, and went on for twenty-nine days. A great many in the city were converted. There was one street leading off from the place where we were holding meetings, where, so many of the merchants became converts that they called it "Christian Alley."

At the end of the twenty-nine days the tent had to be taken down and the work moved back to the street chapel. Then the street chapel proved to be absolutely inadequate. We had to roof over even the yard in front of the chapel in order to accommodate the crowds who came. All this goes to prove that when we attempt great things for God we may expect great things from God. When we lengthen our cords and strengthen our stakes, God will break forth on the right hand and on the left.

It was on the twenty-ninth night that Mr. Su came for the first time. On this night he was several parts drunk. He felt in his pocket and found about twenty dollars there.

SCRIPTURE TESTIMONY
Jesus is able to save to the uttermost
HEBREWS 7:25

He was moved to go over to the railway station, where there were plenty of harlots and gambling-dens, and he was going to have a big blow-out that night. Getting into his Ricksha, he went north through the city and came to the center of it, where he had to turn west to the railway station. Just then he heard an organ playing, and a violin. My wife was at the organ, and my son Wallace was playing the violin. Mr. Su stopped his ricksha and asked: "What sound is that? I never heard a sound like that in China before."

The 'rickshaman replied: "Those are the Christians over in the temple yard. They have a big mat shed there, and have been holding meetings for a month. Didn't you know about it?"

"No," said Mr. Su, "I didn't know about it. I never went near them."

The 'rickshaman continued: "That is an organ, and that is a violin, to help them sing their songs."

Mr. Su said: "I am not going over to the railway station. I am going in here to see this strange sight." He paid his 'rickshaman off and came in. Being half drunk, he was not a bit bashful, so came forward and took a front seat right before me.

That night I was speaking on "This is a faithful saying and worthy of all acceptation, that Jesus Christ came into the world to save sinners, of whom I am chief." I had expected Mr. Hu I-chwang, the famous preacher, to have taken the meeting that night, but he was so ill he could not speak, and I had to take his place. On the spur of the moment I chose that text, and began.

I have often since heard Mr. Su say, in telling about that night, "It was not long before he made me hopping mad." He said that right there before the crowd. With him sitting on the front seat, I talked all about his sins and failures. He could not understand how I came to know all about him. He knew that all I said was true, but it made him angry to feel that I did not distribute it among the crowd, but piled it all up on him. At the close of the meeting I called for decisions. Mr. Su said the thing was so good he supposed that everyone who needed saving would put up his hand, but they didn't. He thought they certainly were a lot of cowards in not accepting a good thing like that, so he just put up his own hand to show them that he was not afraid. A couple of the evangelists went down and invited him to go back with them into the inquiry-room, and he went. That night he died unto sin and commenced to live unto righteousness. Drink was his great curse, but it and tobacco and gambling and vice all dropped out that very night. He commenced to live for the glory of God. How do you account for this change? Is it not that our Saviour is able to save to the uttermost all that come unto God through Him?

Mr. Su's father was a proud Confucian scholar, a B.A. from one of the noted families in the county. The idea of his son disgracing the whole clan by going after these "foreign devils"! He came in a rage and, reviling his son, slapped his face and drove him out of the house. Mr. Su was cut off immediately from his place of employment in the city, where he had been secretary of the electric-light plant. Even his wife turned against him and would not live with him. He came to me and said:

"I am going to follow you all over the world, even if I have to starve for it, that I may learn the secret of that power which has made this amazing change in me. The things that I once loved I now hate; the things that I once hated I now love. In the Boxer year I so hated you, if I could have gotten near you with a knife I would have killed you. Now, somehow, I feel I could die for you."

Mr. Su has been with me ever since. I have never met a more consecrated man in my life. He gets a salary of forty-one Chinese dollars a month, and out of that he keeps an evangelist down in his native city. If Mr. Su were to get a salary of two hundred dollars a month, it would be all the same. He would not have any left. He has a wife and five children, but he never saves anything for the future. He is the most tireless worker I have ever known. I am always dreading lest he break down. He has been converted seventeen years and his knowledge of the Bible is remarkable. I ought to know a good deal about the Bible. When I was five years of age my mother started me to memorize passages in it. It became a habit with me, so that I never could find a Sunday-school teacher who could take time on Sunday to hear all my memory verses. Oh, parents, how much you lose out by not getting the Bible into the memories of your children in the early years!

In the mandarin language of North China we have a new version of the Bible out during the last twenty years. Since it came out I have gone over the New Testament fifty-seven times in Chinese, comparing it with the English version, and I have spent considerable time with the Old Testament, but I would not like to be put on a test examination with Mr. Su. He would beat me every time. I hear him quoting the New Testament, and am amazed. He seems to be able to quote the whole of it, chapter and verse, and much of the Old Testament. I have seen audiences melted as by judgment when he has spoken. I have known a high school of more than a hundred pupils all broken to the utmost, and the teachers as well, and he alone able to guide them.

It was not many years before he won his father, mother, wife, and brothers and sisters. The Su family is one big clan occupying the northeast portion of T'ang yin city. When holding meetings in T'ang-yin I have been astonished at his wonderful influence over those of his clan. It struck me that he was the most influential man in his county, and it was all due to the power of God which attended him.

For many years, in all my evangelistic work in different provinces Mr. Su has gone with me. He is my tried and trusted co-worker in Szepingkai, Manchuria. With him there to take my place, I have every confidence in the result. To save one such man from among China's millions is surely worth while.

How much hinged on that timely gift from the woman in far-away Australia! But for her gift the putting up of that pavilion would have been impossible. Humanly speaking, Mr. Su would have had no possibility of coming into the Kingdom of God at that time. Not only would the results in the lives of many others have been delayed, but multitudes who have since been saved through Mr. Su would also have been hindered in the way of Life Eternal.

XII. GOSPEL TRIUMPHS AMONG SCHOLARS OF

ONE COUNTY

"POTTERY" COUNTY is a county of considerable area in the southwest corner of Chi-li Province. It contains five hundred and seventy towns and villages. In doing missionary work, on entering any county town, my first visit would be to the magistrate, the second to the educational office, then to the various schools.

On one of these occasions, when visiting the educational office in the county town, the inspector of boys' schools for the county invited me over to have dinner with himself and friends next day at noon. I accepted, and took my Bible under my arm. I was cordially received by the inspector, the secretary, and Mr. Shen, the head of the Information Bureau, and others.

When dinner was ended I opened my Bible and commenced to talk with them. At once Mr. Shen, the head of the Information Bureau, challenged me, saying that he had read John Stuart Mill, Darwin, and others, and that he did not believe there was any God, nor heaven nor hell, but that this life ended all. The inspector and others in the room were all alert to see what I would say. Naturally I could not let it pass.

I spoke about creation as we popularly find it, our own solar system, and other suns and systems filling immensity, and asked:

"Is it possible that you believe there is no God when we have all these wonders?"

119

"They all came by chance," he replied. He had the nebular hypothesis at his finger tips and kept insisting that all came by chance.

I went at him again in this way. "There is a railroad west of the city running from Peking to Hankow. Did that come by chance?"

"No, engineers planned and built it, of course."

"Trains run north and south every day. Do they all go by chance? Are these engines run by chance?"

"No, of course," he admitted, "there is an engineer on board."

"Well," I remarked, "if I were on board that train and you could persuade me that there was no engineer in front, I would jump off that train at the risk of breaking my neck, for I know there would be a terrible smash-up sooner or later if it all ran by chance. Of course we all know there are engineers and conductors on all those trains."

Then I mentioned the velocity with which these other suns and systems are going through space and said:

"Do you mean to say they are all running just by chance?" I found, no matter how I talked about creation and its wonders, I could not hold him down to any one point. The inspector and the other friends were all eagerly listening to us.

Then I decided to take up with them the fulfillment of prophecy, and along the line of that remarkable book, *The Wonders of Prophecy*. I said:

"Friend, if in this book of mine I can find things foretold, and if I can find that tens or hundreds or thousands of years afterward there is complete fulfillment, will you not believe that this Book is given to us by an all-wise God?"

"Oh no, all just comes by chance. I don't believe this book is of God at all."

"Well, I will admit that there might be complete fulfillment of a thing once or twice or even five times by chance, but you could not claim that that was possible in scores of cases."

"No," he generously conceded, "of course if you have scores of cases, then my scientific mind would compel me to admit that there must be a guiding mind controlling. But," he went on, "have you got anything like that?"

I answered, "In connection with Christ's first coming to earth we have at least two hundred prophecies all fulfilled."

"I don't believe in Christ," he declared. "I don't believe He was the Son of God. I believe He was a man born of His parents just the same as the rest of us.

"But," I said, "there are many prophecies in this book concerning His second coming, and they will all be fulfilled in time. However, since you do not believe in Christ, I am not going to mention any prophecy concerning Him now. I will just take up the prophecies concerning Tyre and Sidon. Do you know where those cities are?" I asked.

He hesitated and replied: "Well, I really don't know where they are."

At once the inspector and his friends commenced to doubt whether this head of the Information Bureau knew everything "under heaven," as he pretended to. I explained to them where these cities were situated.

"Now," I said, "in my Book here in the twenty-sixth and twenty-seventh chapters of Ezekiel we will find these cities mentioned. The inhabitants of those places despised and mocked at the people of God, the Jews, and God through his prophet Ezekiel foretold what punishment would be meted out to them. We notice here as we read in these chapters that the punishment to be meted out is not the same for both cities. Sidon is to have trouble. She is to keep a continuous existence, apparently, but a troublous one. That is true to history. She has been having trouble down through the centuries but *she still exists*. History has proved it.

"But of Tyre," I continued, "it says that she shall be completely destroyed, and her stones and timbers put into the sea, and the rocks scraped bare so that the fishermen shall spread their nets to dry on them. What then happened in Tyre? Do you know?"

"No," he admitted, "I do not know."

"Nebuchadnezzar," I went on to say, "the great Babylonian monarch, came and besieged Tyre. They kept this great warrior out for two years, getting supplies in by the sea, and Nebuchadnezzar could not starve them out. But the Tyrians saw plainly that they would have to yield in the end, and so they took all their valuables out of the city over to an island about two-thirds of a mile away. Nebuchadnezzar had no ships, and they knew they would be safe there. It is quite certain that he did not get the valuables of that city. Look on down in one of these chapters [Ezek.

29:17-20]. He did not get the treasure in Tyre, but he later got it down in Egypt. And then Nebuchadnezzar sacked the city in his rage and razed it to the ground. But he was not interested in fulfilling prophecy in putting the stones and timbers into the sea, *yet they were put there later in order to fulfill prophecy.* Now would you tell us how they got into the sea, because they did get there?"

"No," he said, "I cannot tell."

Then I went on, while all in the room listened with breathless attention. "One hundred years passed, and still they were there. Two hundred years passed, and still they were there. Two hundred and forty years passed, and still they were there. Then Alexander the First, the great King of Macedon, was marching eastward with a conquering army. The Tyrians, on hearing of this man, sent an embassy to talk peace. Alexander said: (I don't want war with you. All that I ask is that you permit me with my army to go to your capital city. In the meantime the Tyrians had built their capital city on the island. The Tyrians, when they heard this request consulted, and decided it would be safer to keep Alexander on the seashore and not let him over on to the island. They refused and defied Alexander and his army.

"Was a man like that to be balked? No. He ordered his soldiers to take these ruins of Tyre and put them into the sea to make a causeway over to the island. Into the sea those ruins went, but they were not sufficient to make the causeway. Material was scarce, so that even the rocks had to be scraped bare in order to get material enough to build the causeway. Finally Alexander captured that city and blotted it out."

For about twenty minutes Mr. Shen's head had been bowed, and when I finished with the ultimate overthrow of Tyre and the fulfillment of this prophecy, Mr. Shen looked up with tears in his eyes, and said, "I believe there is a God."

The inspector brought his big hand down with a bang on the table, saying, "No other Book in the world is going to save China but this book." Within a year all the men listening to me that day, including Mr. Shen, were converts and had entered the church.

Mr. Shen had tuberculosis, but he earnestly walked with God as long as he lived. Just a few days before he died he attended Sunday service in the chapel. I walked out with him, with my arm over his shoulder, and when I asked, "Mr. Shen, how is it with you? I shall never forget that smile of his as he said, "I will soon be with my Lord and Saviour."

Since then about fifteen or twenty M.A.'s and B.A.'s of that county have turned to God, and many of the government-school teachers. At one time out of the seven government boarding-schools in the county the head masters of five were Christians. The inspector of boys' schools and the inspector of girls' schools became elders in the church, and the ex-treasurer of the county became a deacon.

THE STORY OF LI FU-POA[1]

Among the most noted of these scholar converts was Li Fu-poa. He had the *Pa Kung* degree, which is a very coveted degree in China. Only one such degree is issued every twelve years in a county. No matter how many men compete in this special examination, only one can get this coveted degree. Li Fu-poa gained this degree, and therefore was among a select few in his county. This great scholarship, however, did not save him from the power of the devil. I have often visited his school of seven or eight hundred boys in the county town. He could talk well, as all Chinese scholars can talk, but he lived ill. The fame of the Chinese classics is that they are of a high ethical standard and they are readily quoted by the scholars, but too often they mean nothing to them. Mr. Li would leave his school and go to haunts of vice. The boys all knew it. He was a noted gambler. He could play at dice and cards and mah-jong all at once and win all round. Did you ever hear of mah-jong? It is the worst devil game we have in China. Men have been known in a single night to squander as much as ten thousand dollars on mah-jong. The game was quite popular some years ago on this Christian continent. Once a ship sailing from Shanghai brought over twenty-five tons of mah-jong sets to enable Christian America to glorify the devil by playing that game. The people of this continent either did not know how to play or had not the patience to play it. Many Christian people have gone back to cards instead.

---

1 Pronounced Lee Foo-boa.

Mr. Li finally gave up his school and went as secretary with a noted military leader in Shanghai. There he got big pay but committed big sins. I have heard him say that on an evening when bedtime came he would feel in his pocket to see how much money he had. He would perhaps find twenty-five or thirty dollars there. It was in danger of burning a hole in his pocket if it were not spent that night. He would shake off this wrong feeling, throw off his clothes and get into bed. But the devil would not let him sleep. He would roll around there in bed. That money was surely going to burn a hole in his pocket if not spent, and he would get up and put on his clothes, get into a 'ricksha, and hurry to the center of Shanghai, where there were plenty of gambling-dens and harlot houses. He would have a wild debauch in getting rid of the money in his possession. Then he would come home to rest.

Is not the devil a hard taskmaster? Besides this, he finally got addicted to opium and morphine and cigarettes. He could not get along with less than twenty cigarettes a day.

In 1921, the year after the great famine, my wife and I were with a preaching band, and came to the Pottery town, to hold meetings for eight days. Mr. Li was home at that time, but of course had no intention of coming to our meetings. His father, a B.A., was a convert. I sent my card up to Mr. Li Fu-poa with the message: "I am so busy morning, noon, and night that I have not time to go up to see you. I wish you would come to me." When he came I sat down opposite to him in the guest room. I asked him, "Mr. Li, what might your age be just now?"

"Oh, I am just forty years of age," he answered.

"Certainly you have served the devil well these forty years," I said to his face. "How much longer do you plan to serve him? Has God no rights in your life? From God's Book here I gather that you are heading straight for hell. Can you imagine that when you arrive there you are going to have cigarettes and morphine and opium prepared for you? The craving will be ten thousand times more awful there than it is in this world, but you will find nothing there to ease it."

For some time I talked on the awful fate of the lost. He seemed to be thoroughly aroused, and said, "Well, I shall have to begin to cut it off gradually. It came on me gradually."

"Mr. Li," I replied, "from what you say, you seem to think you can save yourself. If you are able to save yourself, you are certainly the first sinner who ever has been able to do so. A sinner can no more get himself disentangled from his sins than a man can get himself disentangled from a devilfish when the tentacles are all fastened around him." I went on to tell how God's way of saving a sinner was through faith in the Lord Jesus Christ; that all his sins were borne in Christ's own body on the Cross.

In surprise he inquired, "Do you mean to tell me that all I have to do is to believe that Jesus Christ the Son of God died for me on the Cross, and plead His merits with God the Father, in order to be saved from sin?"

"Why, of course! There is no other way. All sinners up to the present have been saved that way. All sinners to the end shall be saved that way. God the Father has no other plan."

For a time he sat and considered, and then deliberately said: "I here and now for all time accept Jesus Christ as my Saviour. I yield to Him." That day Mr. Li ceased from opium, from morphine and from cigarettes, from cards and from vice of every kind. He commenced to live unto righteousness.

I like to take a man like that out of his surroundings, lest he be tempted beyond what he is able to bear. I invited him to come along with us in the preaching band. "In a few days," I told him, "we are moving off to another place. Won't you come with as?"

He agreed: "Yes, I would like to go with you. May I bring my son along?"

"Of course, by all means" we replied. The son was a fine young man about twenty-one. They came, and within a month Mr. Li was one of the ablest preachers in the band. When a scholar of such eminence stood on the platform, the people naturally looked up and took notice. If there was a special occasion with more scholars than usual present, the other Chinese leaders would whisper to me, "Let's get Li Fu-poa forward as soon as possible."

After about two and a half months our work with the band was finished for that season. That last morning Mr. Li and I walked together into the city, eight miles. As we conversed by the way he said: "When we go out again with the preaching band we must divide up into two parties. While one party is taking preaching in turns, the other party must be away in a quiet place praying for the success of the work." That was not bad vision for a babe in Christ two and a half months old! There are men and women who have been Christians for ten, twenty, or thirty years who have not as clear vision as that. They are rarely found at a prayer-meeting, yet the prayer-meeting is the very power-house of the church of God. In most churches these prayer-meetings are very thinly attended. In some churches they have died out altogether. The people of God have lost vision.

I have never met a more humble Christian than Mr. Li Fu-poa. For real haughtiness and proud bearing commend me to an ordinary Chinese scholar. But the grace of God made such a change in Mr. Li that he would do the most menial service for the brethren. He and Mr. Su accompanied me for years in my evangelistic work to different parts, even as far away as Shanghai. In Marshal Feng's army and wherever he went everyone was conscious that here was a spirit-filled man of God.

After he was converted about two years and had been preaching with us, Mr. Li was suddenly seized and thrown into prison. At that time the governor of Chili Province wanted to get some "squeeze" money to fill his coffers, and he thought of the plan of seizing all the well-to-do users of opium and flinging them into prison until they paid the money he demanded. They took no notice of the change that had come in Mr. Li Fu-poa, for he had once been a noted opium-user, and they put him into prison until he would pay his fine. He refused absolutely to pay the fine. When we heard of it we sent word to the magistrate saying that he had been a convert for two years, and that he had ceased using opium and had been preaching with us. The magistrate understood and felt that he had no right to be in prison, but Mr. Li was sent from there to one of the larger cities and was flung into the military prison under the divisional commander.

Many other opium-users were also in the same prison. Mr. Li took his hymn-book and Bible along, naturally. No one knew what his fate might be. He might be taken out and shot any day for refusing to pay the fine. The prison fare at any time is rather scrimped, but these wealthy opium-users were so depressed that even the little that was given them they could not eat. Mr. Li, however, had a clear conscience and a fine appetite, and he said he grew fat while in prison because he ate what others left as well as his own portion. The Christians of his home county became alarmed as to the possible danger of his losing his life, and one of the elders who was the inspector of boys' schools for the county, and one of the deacons who was ex-treasurer, came up to Peking to see me and ask if I could not persuade Marshal Feng to do something for his release. Marshal Feng knew him quite well, because he had preached in the army.

I went right in and saw Marshal Feng. As soon as he heard about what had happened to Mr. Li Ftt-poa, he exclaimed, "That hypocrite of a governor! He is the biggest opium sot in the province. I know the military man that he is under. He is a friend of mine. I persuaded him to trust in the Lord Jesus Christ and he has given up his opium." Immediately the marshall's secretary was called in, and he dictated a letter to this friend, the divisional commander.

As soon as the letter arrived at Taiming this general had Li Fu-poa brought into prison, and he asked, "Are you a Christian?"

"Of course I am!"

"Well, are you not afraid to be a Christian? You are in danger of losing your life now in prison here. Are you not afraid to die?"

"No, I am not."

The general then spoke out: "I am glad to hear you say that because I am a Christian, too. Your friend, Marshal Feng, has sent a letter here about you. You are at liberty."

So with joy Mr. Li went back into the prison to collect his belongings and go home. When he announced to his fellow-prisoners that he was set at liberty and was now going home, they said:

"Well, you may go and take your other things, but you are not to take that Bible and hymn-book. You can buy new ones, but we have received too much comfort from those you have used here to let you take them away."

Later on, when we were on furlough, Mr. Li Fu-poa was out with the preaching band to the west of Changte. He was taken down with scarlet fever. His friends put him on a cart with a heathen driver to bring him in to the hospital at Changte. That cruel fellow dumped him off with his belongings west of the railway. He had to carry his bedding and baggage over half a mile to the hospital. He died next morning. When I heard about it I was heart-broken that a man so young and of such splendid promise should be called home! Had he lived I had visions of thousands in that county turning to God, because he had pupils all over the county and all marveled at the change that had come into the life of their former teacher.

These facts go to prove that scholars can be reached with this Gospel of the Kingdom, and that with scholars as with all others the Word of God is quick and powerful, sharper than any two-edged sword.

XIII. THE ANGEL OF SHANGHAI

"'Tis better to walk in the dork with God

Than to run in the light alone;

Better to follow His voice and His rod,

Than without Him to inarch to a throne"

THE FOLLOWING story of what God can do with a weak, broken human channel, wholly yielded to Him, was told to the writer by one for years closely associated with the subject of this sketch.

SCRIPTURE TESTIMONY
God using circumstances and timing to communicate
ACTS II:II

Towards the close of the last century Cornelia Bonnell, a young American girl attending Vassar College in New York State, heard the call of her needy, neglected sisters in China, and into her heart full of love for the Saviour there came an intense longing to tell them of Him. She was a delicate girl, so frail, indeed, that the years in which she strove to complete her education were years of extreme testing, both physically and financially. The brave, indomitable will and courageous spirit which were so evident in her life later on can be seen by the heroic way she overcame all obstacles to obtaining the best possible training for life's service.

129

It was while she was at Vassar that Miss Bonnell passed through a deep spiritual experience, the story of which I am unable to give; but it was at the time of this experience that she was led to step out in faith and trust for physical strength. No spectacular miracle of healing was granted to her, either then or in the years that followed, but one of the outstanding lessons of her life was how God could and did supply the needed strength to that weak frame as she went forward in quiet faith and performed what appeared to those watching her the humanly impossible.

Graduating from Vassar College, Miss Bonnell took a course in kindergarten work, and later a course of Bible study at the Baptist Theological College, Newton. Then came her application to the Baptist Foreign Mission Board to be sent to China. But, to her dismay, a kind but firm refusal was received. "Full of zeal? No doubt. Well fitted? Yes, but what board would care to take the responsibility of sending one so frail, perhaps to die on the way?" Though baffled, Miss Bonnell kept on praying the Lord to open her way to China. From now on we see His hand working out a plan for her.

Miss Martha Jewell, the head of a school for English- speaking children in Shanghai, hearing of Miss Bonnell, wrote offering her a position in the school as teacher of English and saying she would take the risk of her health. While this was far from what Miss Bonnell had expected, she accepted it as God's opening for her, and on the 25th of December, 1899, landed in Shanghai. Miss Jewells school being closed because of the Christmas holidays, Miss Bonnell stayed for some days at a missionary home.

Having nothing to do and wishing to see something of Shanghai, she started off one day in a 'ricksha. Unable to understand where she wanted him to go, the 'rickshaman took her, of his own accord, down through the district wholly given over to flagrant, indescribable immorality. Crushed with sorrow at what she saw, Miss Bonnell closed her eyes and cried to God: "O my Father, cannot I do something to save these my sisters?" Then and there the answer came back in unmistakable tones, "Except thou bring these with thee, thou canst not see my face." Again she cried, "Give me a sign that this is really Thy call. Lead Miss Jewell to set me free from my three years' contract with her. And do this without my saying anything to her of Thy call."

The following Sunday, while Miss Jewell was attending the morning service in the Union Church, a strong impression came to her that Miss Bonnell should be set free for work among the women of the red-light district. So definite and strong was this impression that Miss Jewell called Miss Bonnell to her room that same afternoon and told her what was in her mind. To her surprise, Miss Bonnell began to weep. When Miss Jewell assured her she would not urge her to take up such a work, Miss Bonnell, with her face radiant through her tears, exclaimed, "I was weeping for joy at the way the Lord has revealed His will."

As the shadows of evening were lengthening for the last time in the old century, a missionary prayer-meeting, held in the Union Church, Shanghai, came to a close. Five women tarried behind as the others passed out, and stood together in a darkening passageway. They did not realize it at the time, but they represented five distinct missionary organizations—Presbyterian, Baptist, Methodist, Anglican, and China Inland Mission. They were drawn together by a common impulse, a common burden which had lain on their hearts for months (in at least one case for years), namely, the crying need for some one to work among the thousands of outcast women and girls within the Foreign Settlement of Shanghai. As each prayed, the burden was for God to send such a worker and of His own fitting and choosing. Little did they dream that God had His channel already called and waiting to know His will, even then in Shanghai.

Later, when meeting Miss Bonnell, not one of the five women who had met that New-year's Eve hesitated in accepting her as God's chosen one; and through the hard uphill years that followed they stood behind her, helping in every possible way. From the beginning of the work, however, all recognized and bowed to Miss Bonnell's remarkable gifts of organization and initiative. From the purely human standpoint, no one could have been more unfitted to take up such a work than Cornelia Bonnell. Her extreme youth, barely twenty-one, her frail, almost emaciated frame, her total lack of knowledge in Chinese customs, and the necessity for her to spend years of strenuous study in a most unhealthy climate before being able to speak Chinese freely—these were some of the reasons why for years public opinion was against her. But Miss Bonnell could say with

Paul, "None of these things move me." She had caught the vision, had heard God's call which gave her the ever-present realization that God was with her. This undoubtedly was the secret of Miss Bonnell's wonderful calm and power when facing both foreign and Chinese lawyers in the Mixed Court of Shanghai, pleading the cases of girls who had fled to her for protection. Her fiercest fights and hardest experiences came in her dealings with those trained men of the law from *Britain* and *America* who, for the sake of a paltry gain in money, allowed themselves to be the hired agents of the girls "owners."

It must be understood that in stepping out into this work Miss Bonnell and the few standing with her had no financial backing; they looked only to the Lord for the solving of every problem, and there were many. A Chinese house in an alleyway off one of Shanghai's busy roads was secured. Here Miss Bonnell went to live, taking with her one girl who had been reclaimed some years before. From the first the door was kept on the latch night and day. Over the door in large attractive Chinese characters were the words, THE DOOR OF HOPE. Then came a time of severe testing. For months Miss Bonnell waited and prayed for the girls over whom she yearned with heart-breaking sorrow, but in vain, for not one sought the refuge open to them. Then the frail frame gave way and she was carried to the home of a faithful friend. For weeks her life hung in the balance. Then, one day, she insisted on rising and returning to the Home. Surely the Divine Hand led her in this step, for *that very night* about midnight a timid knock was heard, and the first of the many hundreds who were to come entered the Door of Hope, was eagerly welcomed and *loved* into a new life. Love became the watchword of all who joined in this work.

This is not a history of the Door of Hope—that would require a book in itself—but simply an attempt to follow the divine miracle working in the life of this truly remarkable woman. For sixteen years she was spared to live such a life of unselfish devotion, attempting and accomplishing such outstandingly great things that she came to be called by some who knew her, "The Angel of Shanghai." Public opinion turned in her favor and the time came when one of the four Homes was actually supported by the Chinese themselves. Her years of pleading in the Mixed Court were rewarded by a law which gave the Door of Hope the right to keep a woman or girl under its protection from her "owners" till her case could pass before the Mixed Court. Miss Bonnell lived to see the work of her fallen sisters in Shanghai thoroughly founded, with a Receiving Home, a First-year Home, an Industrial Home, a Home for Children, also a Sanatorium. The income required to keep the work going reached into tens of thousands of dollars annually. But God never failed to send in what was needed. A large staff of workers joined Miss Bonnell as time passed. Then, when her work as founder and pioneer was finished, the call came, and on October 16, 1916, she passed into the glory.

Her life was a beautiful, perfect example of our Saviour's words to Paul, "My strength is made perfect in weakness."

In closing this brief sketch it may not be out of place to tell just two stories which will illustrate how the work so faithfully founded by Miss Bonnell has continued.

Some years after Miss Bonnell's death, Dr. Goforth and I were passing through Shanghai on our way to Canada. As usual, we went over to see our friends of the Door of Hope. I was asked to speak to the girls, and I can still recall the thrill I felt as I witnessed the eager, wistful faces and tear-dimmed eyes with which they received my message. A little later Miss Morris asked me to go with her to the Door of Hope Hospital. On the way Miss Morris told me they had many, many sad, tragic cases; then she added, "The one I want you to pray for today is perhaps the crudest, saddest case we have ever known." As we entered a ward, I noticed it was as clean and carefully kept as a ward in a hospital at home. As we drew near a certain bed the look on the face of the girl who lay upon it appalled me. She was deathly pale, and her eyes were staring at me with a look of awful terror. Around her was wrapped a sheet which she held fast to her chest, the hands and arms inside. Unable to take her hand, I gently stroked her brow, endeavoring to show by every look the intense sympathy and sorrow I felt. But each stroke on her brow caused her to shrink from me in increasing terror. Miss Morris led me away, and together we prayed for the poor girl, crushed in body and mind. Miss Morris told me there was absolutely no hope for the girl, either mentally or physically, unless God worked a miracle for her in answer to prayer—as He has often done in the past," she concluded.

Several years later we were again passing through Shanghai, and again came a visit to the Door of Hope. As soon as I met Miss Morris I asked about the poor girl I have just described. "Did she die?" I asked, with my little faith. "Oh, no!" was the reply. "She fully recovered, and became one of our sweetest Christians. She is now at the Nanking Bible School in training for work as a Bible woman."

In the summer of 1928 we were again in Shanghai. The hour spent at the Door of Hope we can never forget. Story after story of God's wonderful goodness to them all was told. At last we rose to say farewell, when Miss Bailey added, eagerly, "Oh, sit down, There is just one more story we *must* tell." The following is what was then told us:

SCRIPTURE TESTIMONY
God's work will not lack God's supply
PHILIPPIANS 4:19

During the disturbances and riots of 1926-27 in Shanghai, the Door of Hope was forced from one place to another, seeking refuge and safety. At last they found themselves in quarters so congested that three girls had but one single bed. The hot weather came on, and as the days and weeks passed the poor girls suffered greatly till Miss Abercrombie realized something must be done. Every effort was made to secure, by renting, a place immediately adjoining them. It was vacant, had a large garden and a building just suited to their needs, but the owner was a wealthy Chinese who absolutely refused to let them have the place at any price, saying he had no need of the money and if he had he would not let the place to foreign devils." At last, when things came to a point of desperate extremity, Miss Abercrombie called all the workers, Chinese and foreign, and all the girls, together to pray unitedly for the Lord to undertake for them. They had been on their knees some time praying when the telephone rang and Miss Bailey rose to receive the message. It was from the owner of the property for which they had been praying, and the message said the man had changed his mind and they could have the place when they pleased. Miss Bailey returned, and when a prayer ceased said, "You need not pray for the place. The man has given it to us." Thus, as when Isaiah wrote the words, the promise is true, "Before they call I will answer and while they are yet speaking I will hear."

XIV. THE BETHEL MISSION, SHANGHAI

"Faith, mighty faith the promise sees

And looks to God alone!

Laughs at impossibilities- and says

It shall be done!"'

A WORK OF FAITH

THE BETHEL mission was founded by Miss Hughes, an American lady, and Dr. Mary and Dr. Phoebe Stone, two Chinese ladies educated in America, both graduates of Johns Hopkins University. They were all connected with a mission in Kiu-kiang, Kiangsi Province.

A question of doctrine came up upon which Miss Hughes could not conscientiously agree with the stand taken by her mission. Consequently, she sent in her resignation. Dr. Mary Stone and her sister, Dr. Phoebe, were in full accord with the step Miss Hughes had taken and they too sent in their resignations.

When Miss Hughes and Dr. Mary Stone wound up their affairs on leaving Kiu-kiang, they found they had only fifty dollars on hand with which to start a new mission. They traveled downriver as cheaply as possible, planning to start a new work in Shanghai. On looking up accommodation in Shanghai they found that a single month for room and board would require half their money. Besides, they did not know what day Dr. Phoebe with thirty nurses in training would also come downriver. Just then some one said to them, "Why don't you get the ex-ambassador house on Arsenal Road?"

The ambassador while in France married a French wife, and brought her out to Shanghai and built a mansion for her. Some months after taking up their residence in their new home it was said that a ghost came one night and put his hand on this Frenchwoman, and she pined away and died. Others who rented the house, it was said, met with the same fate. The reputation of the house became so bad as "haunted" that no one would have anything to do with it. This friend said, "If you are prepared to risk the ghost, you may get the house cheap." The ladies replied, "We are not afraid of ghosts. What we are after is a cheap house that will accommodate all our party." The house was secured. The ladies declared later that while they did not find any ghosts there, they did find lots of dirt, flies, and mosquitoes.

Just after the house was secured, Dr. Phoebe with her thirty nurses arrived, and the girls were accommodated in the top story. The caretaker assured them that there really was a ghost. The girls believed the story enough to always keep a light burning during the night. One night a girl awoke. A strange feeling came over her and she glanced toward the head of the stairway, and true enough there was the ghost. With outstretched hand he moved slowly towards her. She was paralyzed with terror and could not scream. She thought her time had come. But instead of the ghost putting his hand upon her head as she had expected, he put it on her purse lying beside it. Then she screamed, and her cries wakened the other girls. Soon all were up in wild alarm. They heard the ghost with heavy footfalls making speed down the stairway. Then the caretaker, cook, and servants appeared with lanterns and weapons to find the ghost or the disturber, but there was no trace of him. Next day the ladies put their heads together and said, "It would not surprise us if our ghost had his abode in the caretaker's room." They secured a key which unlocked his door and found there stolen stuff and duplicate keys for every room in the house. That day the caretaker was dismissed, and the ghost was seen no more.

The work branched out in all directions. Several automobiles were kept going constantly. The doctors were busy in their hospitals and with calls from all over the city. Other workers joined them and they carried on evangelistic effort in several of the large factories employing thousands of women and girls.

Such a rapidly increasing work as this would of necessity mean a proportionate increase in expenditure. Where, then, did the money come from? We sincerely hope that

SCRIPTURE TESTIMONY
God answers prayer
LUKE 18:7 · JOHN 15:7 · ACTS 12:5 · JAMES 5:15

some day either Dr. Mary Stone or Miss Hughes will write the story themselves of God's marvelous faithfulness in supplying the funds necessary to carry on. The following may serve to throw some light on this side of the work.

On one occasion when new buildings were being erected, by a certain date a sum of money had to be paid to the contractors. No funds were on hand to meet this payment. The two ladies prayed daily that the money might come, but up to the very day the payment was due no money had reached them. While at breakfast the ladies decided between them that while Dr. Mary Stone went to her morning clinic, Miss Hughes would go to the American post office in Shanghai. Miss Hughes took with her all the necessary papers for conducting the business with the contractor *when she received the money!* On inquiring at the post office for mail a letter was handed her inclosing a check sufficient to meet the payment and about fifty cents over!

Again, as the work increased the need for a telephone became imperative, for the Bethel Mission was situated about two-thirds of the way to the Arsenal, which was at least five miles from the center of the city. Every effort to get a telephone connection met with failure. To have their own connection made with the city was costly. At last the ladies had special prayer, believing that He who had undertaken for them so often would again find a way to meet their need. A day or two later, when motoring to her city clinic, a man motioned for Dr. Mary Stone to stop. He said: "I hear you are wanting a telephone put in your place. If you go to such and such a man, I think he could put you on the right track." She did so, and it was found the telephone connection with the Arsenal actually passed the front gate of the Bethel Mission and it was the simplest matter to make the necessary connections there.

When in Shanghai on one occasion, my wife and I were invited to take supper at the Bethel Mission. After supper I was asked to speak to their assembly. There must have been about one hundred and fifty present, nurses and others.

Dr. Mary Stone said, "There are many of the nurses and others unconverted. I hope you will make a special effort to reach them."

I spoke on the text, "Quench not the Holy Spirit." At the close I called for decisions, and dozens responded. I came to the conclusion that they did not understand my northern dialect, and that it was only the Christians who had stood up. Dr. Stone said: "Now I am going to give out a hymn, and after the singing of the hymn I want you to make another effort to get decisions."

I replied: "Dr. Stone, you see they do not understand my language. When I called for decisions, only your Christians stood up."

"No," said the doctor, "it wasn't the Christians, it was the unsaved whom we were longing for, and there are others too who have not yet decided."

Again I tried, and more came out on the Lord's side.

That evening Miss Chou, from a millionaire family, was indisposed and was not down at the meeting. (Her grandfather had been the late viceroy of Nanking. While an official in Shantung he had come to be on friendly terms with Rev. Dr. Timothy Richards. He visited France and Britain. In the Boxer year he held an official post in Szechwan Province. The governor, along with the chief military man of the Province, decided to massacre all the foreigners with the native Christians. Mr. Chou remonstrated, saying, "I have been in the West; I know the enormous power which these Western nations wield. Carry out your proposals and you destroy China. These nations will unite and come in force and take everything from us." The warning was sufficient. No missionary was killed and no native Christians massacred in that province.)

The nurses who had decided that evening for the Lord Jesus Christ, on going up to their sleeping-quarters told Miss Chou that they had all decided to serve the Lord Jesus. They said: "He spoke so we couldn't help it. He told us that the Spirit of God was always striving with us to lead us to accept Christ Jesus as our Lord and Saviour, and he went on to say that as long as we failed to decide to follow the Lord Jesus we were quenching the Holy Spirit." Miss Chou in alarm put on her kimona and came down to see Dr. Mary Stone and Miss Hughes. She said:

"How can I possibly serve the Lord Jesus? It is coming right on to New-year's time. We are expecting our cousins to come from Peking, Tsinanfu, and other places. I know when they arrive they will just be gambling all the time. Our stepmother has taught all of us girls to gamble. Our stepmother would come in of an evening, throw down a hundred dollars on the table, apportion an equal share to each of us girls, and she would say, 'Now, girls, set to. Whoever can win all this money can reckon it as her own. If I now give my heart to the Lord Jesus, how am I going to withstand the temptation? And yet if I do not, according to what Mr. Goforth has said, I sin the sin of quenching the Holy Ghost."

"Well," said the ladies, "you know what God has said. We leave it with your own conscience as to how you are going to treat him."

Dr. Stone invited me to come back on Sunday morning and again speak to them. Do what I would I could not get away from the words, "If any man will come after me, let him deny himself, take up his cross, and follow me." Sitting right before me on the front seat was a very comely young woman of about twenty years of age. She seemed to listen with her whole soul. When I called for a decision she stood up and said, "I accept the Lord Jesus Christ as my Saviour." This was Miss Chou. Then she prayed, saying: "Heavenly Father, I have now yielded my life to Thee. You know what a hard time I am going to have in a few days during the New-year, but You are Omnipotent, You are able to keep me from falling. Do enable me to give a good confession for my Lord." New year's came on and the cousins arrived, but Miss Chou with the aid of her Lord carried things His way. They hadn't any appetite for gambling. The evening after all the friends had departed, her stepmother, brother, and youngest sister being in the room, the brother said: "Well, life doesn't seem to be worth living. Think of a man as great as our grandfather; he was not allowed to continue forever. I have in mind to give it all up, to go and spend the rest of my days in a monastery in the mountains."

"Shame!" said Miss Chou, "to think of carrying out such a selfish idea, when multitudes in the world are perishing because they lack the salvation which we can bring to them. My life is to be spent in serving Jesus Christ for the salvation of others."

Her young sister, a lass of fourteen, with dancing eyes of merriment, spoke up and said, "My sister's God for me, too."

Some months later we were invited along with Mr. Su and Mr. Li Fu-poa to conduct eight days' special meetings at the Bethel Mission. My two addresses each day were aimed for the deepening of the spiritual life, while the Chinese brethren gave the evangelistic addresses for the outsiders. A hundred and fifty men and women gave in their names as inquirers. The eldest sister of Miss Chou, who is married to the wealthiest Chinese in Shanghai, was so far convalescent that she could attend our meetings. One day she stood up and avowed her faith in the Lord Jesus Christ. It naturally made a very deep impression upon the audience. At the close of the meeting it was a moving sight to see these two sisters, with the tears running down their cheeks, going away with arms around each other's necks.

An unusual incident happened during the days of the meetings. One day a dog came in to the Bethel Mission compound, prowling around for something to eat. On the rubbish heap he could find not even a bone, but there was an old rent Chinese Bible there, with both covers torn away. The dog took the book in his mouth and marched into a large encampment across the way. The soldiers had often seen a dog with a bone in his mouth, but never before a dog with a book in his mouth. They ran him down and captured the book. They were delighted to find it to be in their own language, and day by day groups of men would gather around the book and some one would read. The officers noticed it and came to see. They, too, became interested. One of the officers said: "This book evidently is not complete. I shouldn't wonder if we went over to the Bethel Mission we might get a complete book there." One evening an officer, surrounded by a number of soldiers, stood up in the meeting and related the incident of the dog and the torn book, and asked if they hadn't a complete Bible, and naturally it was freely given to him. Next day the colonel sent the major over to say, "If you can get permission from the general above us, you are at liberty to come into this encampment to preach as much as you will."

Among the hundred and fifty decisions mentioned above, forty were Manchurian students who had been sent down to study at the Arsenal. There were over eighty of these students, and I gave each one a present of a New Testament.

By-and-by the owner of the big house became convinced that the former troublesome ghost was not dangerous any longer. He immediately ran the rent up sky high. In the meantime some one had given money enough to the Bethel Mission for the building of a high school. The ladies moved over into the top of this building to live. But schools are anything but restful places, so the ladies prayed that the Lord would give them a suitable home to take the place of the haunted house. A letter came from a Christian gentleman in America. He wrote: "My wife always took a great interest in your work. She died while we were traveling in India. I want to build a suitable memorial to her. What do you need in the way of a building?" They wrote back of their need for a home. His reply was, "Go ahead and build as fine a residence as you think you need, furnish it with the very best furniture, spare no expense, and I shall meet the bill."

In the spring of 1924 I had a few days in Shanghai before the sailing of our boat. I was able to give the Bethel Mission about a dozen addresses. Sixty-odd professed conversion. I baptized thirty-four on the closing Sunday. Admiral Startin of the British Navy, and Mr. Hoste, were present. Both said this work of the Bethel Mission was the finest piece of the Lord's work they had seen. Mr. Hoste said to the leaders, "From this time on you go down on my prayer list."

My wife has a pet mission in Shanghai—The Door of Hope. I, too, have a pet one; it is the Bethel Mission!

XV. MARSHAL FENG YU-HSIANG

AN UNFINISHED SKETCH

FENG YU-HSIANG might justly be called "the mystery man of China." No man of the present time has suffered more, and no man has defended himself less, from

SCRIPTURE TESTIMONY
Lay down one's life for another
JOHN 15:12-13 · EPHESIANS 5:2 · I JOHN 3:16-18

a propaganda of bitterness organized against him throughout the world. Yet no man, I believe, ranks higher in the affection and esteem of the Chinese people. For obvious reasons, this is only a limited sketch of Marshal Feng.

This great man was born in 1881, of poor parents. The lack of means kept him from getting a good education. He revered his parents. I have never heard him speak of his father without noticing that his eyes filled with tears. He joined the army at fifteen years of age and at once commenced to improve himself by studying at night.

In 1900, the Boxer year, he was told off with his company to go down to the south suburb of Paotingfu. The Boxers were gathered there to massacre the American Board missionaries and their converts. On arriving at the gate of the mission he heard Miss Morrell pleading with the Boxers not to massacre all the believers. She pointed out that they had done great good in medical work and other ways, helping the Chinese, and urged that for this reason their lives should be spared.

145

The Boxers said, "No, we must destroy all."

Then Miss Morrell replied: "Why destroy all? Kill me and let the others go. I am ready to die for them."

The young soldier said that this went like a knife-thrust to his heart. He couldn't keep back the tears. He had never imagined that any human being would have been willing to give his or her life as a ransom for others. He noticed that some of the soldiers and some of the older Boxers were affected by this offer, and these urged that all should be spared. The young men among the Boxers, however, said that nothing but the lives of all would satisfy them. For the time being, the persuasion of the soldiers and the older Boxers prevailed. Miss Morrell was allowed to go back into the compound. Soon she and the others fled through the rear gate and tried to escape, but they were soon overtaken and all massacred.

Right after that Feng's company was ordered up to the north suburb of the city. The Presbyterian missionaries were located there. On arrival, the soldiers found the Boxers gathered in great force and setting fire to the house. It was a two-story building with verandas above and below. The missionaries were all up on the second veranda. The young soldier said he saw one man with a child in his arms, walking up and down. Even when the smoke and flames were curling up around them, no one seemed to be afraid. They just died there. Feng was astonished, and never was able to shake off these two incidents until he himself accepted Jesus Christ as his Lord and Saviour.

Feng Yu-Hsiang's final decision came in the end of 1911, at a meeting conducted by Dr. John R. Mott, and he was baptized by Rev. Liu Fang in the Methodist Episcopal Church. At the time he was a major in the army. His general called him in and remonstrated, but Major Feng pressed the need of salvation so strongly upon the general that in order to get rid of him he said, "You can do as you like."

My first contact with Feng, then a general, was in the Province of Hunan, in 1919. He invited my wife and myself to spend about ten days with him. By that time the Christian movement had spread throughout the brigade among hundreds of the officers and men, and among their wives and daughters. We had two meetings a day in a large theater. One day especially the Spirit of God so mightily moved upon their hearts that from the general down all were in tears and sins were being confessed on every side. These men were not like children, but had gone through several campaigns and had faced death repeatedly; but now their hearts melted like wax under the conviction of the Holy Spirit. They all declare that a mighty spiritual impetus was given to the army at that time. During those days I baptized 507 officers and men.

Everything that we saw and heard in General Fang's army gave us the impression that it was a genuinely spiritual movement. All the missionaries we met in that part of Hunan had the same conviction. Among many other things, they told us of a time when drought threatened everything. General Feng assembled his brigade and announced to all the city that they were going to pray for rain. He first called upon the priests and nuns of the Buddhist and Taoist sects to lead off in prayer. They pleaded to be excused, as that was not in their line. Then General Feng called upon different officers to pray for rain. He himself prayed. That night there was a great rain and famine was averted.

Fifteen months later the brigade had arrived in Sin-yangchou, South Honan. The general again invited me to come and assist them. On our arrival he said, "Remember your chief work is not to try to convert the rank and file of my army, but to use your strength in trying to get all my officers filled with the Spirit of God, for as soon as that takes place the lowest private in the army will feel the effect of it."

One night I heard him addressing a large body of soldiers. He said: "Men, we are soldiers of the Lord Jesus Christ. When we came here we were sorely tempted. There were at least three hundred harlots here when we arrived. I knew if I allowed them to remain here you would be tempted, and so would the young students sent here to the high school. I spoke to the local officials and gentry, to have all these women sent away. When the officials saw I was determined, they pleaded that I would allow at least one half of the women to remain. To drive all away would be an act too drastic and would give offense, they claimed. I said, 'No, all must go.' As your leader I hold myself responsible for your welfare. I also hold myself responsible to the parents of this county who have sent their sons up to high school. Therefore I gave strict orders that all should go, and that within five days, and they went."

On another occasion during those days I was addressing an audience of several hundred officers and non-commissioned officers, the general sitting among them. During the address I suddenly asked, "General, would you mind telling us what you were like nine years ago, before you trusted yourself to the Lord Jesus Christ as Saviour?" He slowly arose and answered, "I certainly was a devil in those days; I had a demon temper. Even if an officer offended me, I reviled him and boxed his ears. At that time my men all hated me and would have knifed me if they had dared. Then Jesus came into my heart and took control. He shed abroad His divine love there. Since then I have ruled with love, not by bad temper, and I assure you tonight that all my men would die for me."

I believe he said the truth. He has the most remarkable control of men that I have ever known.

For their Christmas celebration in 1920 a high platform was erected. The general and the chief officers and the local missionaries were on the platform, and around them were massed nine thousand soldiers, besides at least ten thousand citizens. The hymns, the prayers, and the speeches were all "Glory to God in the Highest" for the gift of His Son. Perhaps the world over that day there was not such a Christmas celebration.

For several months, on and off, I was working with the army. During the weeks just previous to their moving to Shensi Province we held meetings in a large theater. There were three meetings a day, all different troops. Each time the theater was crammed with about two thousand men. My meeting was always at seven in the morning. Chang Chih-chiang was my chairman. One morning he seemed unusually moved. He addressed the men, saying:

"It is strange that when we were heathen we never realized a sense of shame when we were found kneeling before the gods in the temples or if there was a shrine by the wayside. We knelt there and we never minded, no matter how many were looking on. It is only since we have become followers of the Lord Jesus Christ that we are ashamed to be seen on our knees. Men, we know that this ought not to be. Imagine being ashamed of Him Who gave His life a ransom for us!"

Then, kneeling down before that great audience, Colonel Chang poured out his heart in one of the most moving prayers I have ever listened to. Every moment I expected he would break down and weep. At the close he stepped over to me and took my hand and said: "I am going to give up soldiering. I am going out preaching with you. You will reach the civilians and I will reach the military, and we'll go all over the land testifying to our Saviour. I am going right over today to ask Marshal Feng to set me free." He mounted his horse and rode over to headquarters.

"I, too," said General Feng, "would like to give up soldiering and go preaching. For the present I can't spare you. Orders have just come from Peking that our brigade must escort the new military governor into Shensi Province."

The next day was Sunday. We commenced our service at half past six in the morning. We went on until half past six in the evening, with a short interval for breakfast at ten o'clock. General Feng sat at one end of a long table, and his wife at the other. In between were missionaries and their wives and children, and colonels and other officers. That day we baptized 960 officers and men. About twenty came at a time. There was always a colonel holding the bowl of water. I would pass down the line baptizing each one in the name of the Father, the Son, and the Holy Spirit. Just as I reached the last one in the line, Colonel Chang Chih-chiang with his little organ would start up. "O happy day that fixed my choice," etc., or "Come to my heart, Lord Jesus, there is room in my heart for Thee." As these men were going back to their seats another lot were coming forward, and Lu Chung-lin was arranging them in line.

Four thousand six hundred and sixty-six officers and men partook of communion, in eleven different companies, the room being capable of accommodating only several hundred at a time. All who took part that day truly seemed to have the joy of the Lord as their strength—no one seemed impatient; no one seemed weary. Next day they moved off to Shensi.

During the months at Sinyangchou everything said and done impressed me that this was a Christian movement of the most genuine sort. All the missionaries of that provincial center seemed to agree with me.

A year later General Feng became military governor of Honan Province. Shortly afterwards I visited him. He wished to make arrangements for the special meetings we were to hold. After supper the general mounted his bicycle and I took a 'ricksha; we went around to look over the several theaters to fix on a suitable audience-room.

Governor Feng kept everyone busy around him. On a Sunday morning there would be fourteen different places where religious services were held among the regiments of his army. At that time his army had increased to twenty-five thousand men. I generally spoke in a building seating fifteen hundred men. These were all believers, officers, non-commissioned officers, and men.

Governor Feng had everything in that provincial capital run on Christian lines. You could almost imagine you were in Christian Toronto. One of his many training-schools was for provincial police. One day when a great number of men were baptized I took part in baptizing eighty-four policemen. His aim was to have every policeman in the province a follower of Jesus Christ. It might be good for the many if all the police of London, New York, and Chicago were followers of the Lord Jesus Christ.

When General Feng had put in about six months as military governor of Honan his jealous friends took action to have him dismissed. The plausible pretext was promotion to Peking, but the general knew it was an Irish promotion. I called on him to say farewell the evening before his departure. First thing he asked:

"Have you had supper?"

"No, but I am going right back to Mr. Joyce's for it." "No, you shall have supper here. I have just had mine, but yours shall be brought in, and while you are eating I am going to chat with you."

It was very evident that General Feng was feeling keenly his dismissal from the province. With deep feeling he said to me: "As I see it, it will be impossible for me to support my army in Peking. Suppose they starve my army away from me, as I think they plan to do, would you be willing that I should go with you for say four years, that I may learn all of the Bible that you know, so that I may go out and help save my fellow-countrymen?"

"General," I replied, "don't be uneasy. If God Almighty did not permit your leaving the province, all the devils in hell could not get you out. Go up to Peking with an easy mind; train your army to the utmost; leave nothing to chance, not even the shoelaces; put your trust wholly in the Living God and keep out of the rotten politics up there. Then when God's time of opportunity comes he will make use of you."

On the following day, as they were passing through Chengchou, Chiang, the chief of staff, came in with the issue of the local paper. The editor knew that he could say now what he liked about General Feng, because the general was out of the governorship. The chief of staff said:

"Why, General Feng, just listen to these charges that are made against you in this paper. Let me reply to him and his ears will tingle."

General Feng answered with a wave of his hand, "Get thee behind me, Satan."

There was a time of drought while General Feng was governor of Honan. The people had paraded their gods around and used every possible means to induce them to

> SCRIPTURE TESTIMONY
>
> *Elijah, a normal human being, prayed for rain*
>
> JAMES 5:17

send rain. It was all in vain; everything was perishing. In this extremity Marshal Feng announced that his army would assemble and pray for rain. People by the tens of thousands came out to see. After praying that evening, there was a slight shower, but not nearly enough; next day it poured. Surely Marshal Feng and his men had more than the ordinary faith when they could pray for rain in Hunan Province and get it, and pray for rain in Honan Province and get it. All that I saw, all that I heard while I was with his army in Honan Province led me to believe that the movement was truly Christian. I emphasize this point because some have questioned the genuineness of Marshal Feng's conversion.

After the army moved to Peking I spent a good deal of time with them. Sometimes supplies were very straitened. The men for weeks on end had not enough to eat. It was noticeable that their cheeks were becoming more hollow day by day, yet I never was among a more happy or contented lot of men. They knew that their commander even in times of plenty ate the same coarse fare that they did. I have often eaten at the same table with the marshal, but never have I seen him eating bread made of wheat flour. It was always of the coarse grains that the common soldiers had to live on. Months on end I have been among these men, and never saw a man smoking, never smelled liquor on their breaths, never did I hear them swearing or see them fighting. Never once did I find men playing cards or gambling. All manner of useful trades were being taught them. Talk about social service! The best sample of social service I ever saw was there in that great encampment south of Peking. The aim of Marshal Feng was that, when through age or other reasons his men must be dismissed from the army, they would have a reliable trade whereby they might make a decent living. Lieutenants and all below them had to learn these trades.

Marshal Feng's conviction was that by having all his soldiers learn a trade he would do away with banditry. "For example," he said, "our people must always wear socks. An ex-soldier with ordinary ability can make a dollar a day with his little knitting-machine. That means he has a secure income of thirty dollars a month. I care not what inducement a bandit leader may offer to such a man, he is not going to be foolish enough to give up a certain livelihood to take the risks of a bandit. Our bandits are mainly ex-soldiers; therefore, have all our soldiers learn suitable trades and we automatically abolish banditry."

Such was not the vogue in other Chinese armies. Surely the root from which all this social service sprang was Christianity. Some people call Marshal Feng a hypocrite. Well, I only know that morning by morning at half past five o'clock he and I studied the Scriptures together. Hypocrites, as a rule, are not found so early at their Bibles.

Once when Marshal Feng was in the Peking hospital for an operation, General Chang Chih-chiang and I called in to chat with him. While we were there, General P'an, who had charge of aviation for China, called. On being introduced to me he said: "Isn't it astonishing what Marshal Feng has done in his army of thirty thousand men? He has molded them into the model army of China. Other armies are constantly mutinying, but General Feng's men won't mutiny even if they starve to death. It amazes us."

On the little table by his head was Marshal Feng's Bible. It was a well-marked Bible, too. How many of my readers have the courage to take a large Bible into a public hospital with them? Remember, this is what we choose to call "heathen China," and here is Marshal Feng with his big Bible along. Reaching out, I took the Bible and held it up in my hand, saying, "General P'an, this is God's Book. Marshal Feng and his officers and men believe what God says in this Book, and they obey His commandments. Therefore they are not only the model army of China, but of the world." Both Marshal Feng and General Chang said, "True, true, we owe everything to this Book."

Marshal Feng at Peking invited Christian leaders to come and work in his army, as he did in other places. He sent a big truck in for these workers every Sunday morning. Modernists took advantage of it and came out and preached doubt. On a certain Sunday morning, after I had spoken to about fifteen hundred men of the Eighth Brigade, I was sitting chatting with General Li Ming-Chung. One of the chaplains came in and said:

"General, we are finding difficulty in getting the men of a certain battalion out to service."

"How does that come about?" inquired the general.

The chaplain answered: "Several Sundays ago one of these modernists came before them, saying, 'I am going to speak to you from John's Gospel. We scholars have found out that there is a great deal of error in this Gospel. Not a little of it is only tradition. Nevertheless, there are some good things in it, and I am going to talk to you about these good things.' The men say: 'We are sitting there on the ground in the swirling dust and at times in the swirling snow; we have received no benefit from the teaching and we don't want to go any more.'" General Li, coming down with a bang on the table, declared: "We have enough Chinese doubts to contend with in the minds of our men already without importing doubts from abroad. That thing must be stopped."

Later Marshal Feng talked with me about it; and since he could not distinguish good from bad, the truck was sent no more for preachers.

On one occasion Marshal Feng told me that he had invited a noted Hanlin scholar to come and teach the Chinese classics to his officers, who had missed early educational advantages, and he felt they ought now to have a chance. This scholar,

SCRIPTURE TESTIMONY
Believers are the aroma of Christ to those around them
2 CORINTHIANS 2:14-16

though he had been a governor of a province, never enriched himself by
"squeezing" the people, consequently at fifty-eight years of age he was a
poor man. In reply to Marshal Feng's invitation he said he would come
on three conditions: first, since, he was a follower of the great Confucius,
he would have nothing to do with Jesus, the Western Sage; second, since
he had smoked all his days, he must be allowed to smoke when he came
to the camp to teach; third, he would not presume to teach Marshal Feng
on account of his high rank.

Said the Marshal, "I was so keen to get him that I readily agreed to
these three conditions. Thus you can see how my mouth is closed. I wish
you would try to save him. But for the life of you, do not hint to him
that I put you up to it."

"All right" I replied. "I'll find a way." I asked the chief chaplain to introduce me, but said, "As soon as you see us two talking freely, you make an
excuse and go away and leave us alone."

When we two were alone, Mr. Wang, the Hanlin scholar, said, "I came
here on three conditions, and he mentioned the three. In speaking of the
second condition, that he must be allowed to smoke, he said, "Coming
here among thirty thousand young men, and never seeing one of them
idly wasting money in smoking tobacco, how dare I, a follower of the great
Sage, set them such a bad example through my indulgence? Therefore I
quit it." Some prominent followers of the Lord Jesus Christ are not so
careful about their outward conduct as this Confucian scholar. Marshal
Feng had not a single rule against smoking or drinking or gambling, but
the men followed his splendid example.

Once Marshal Feng remarked to me: "Probably you think I have rules
against smoking, drinking, and gambling in my Army."

I replied, "Judging by the excellent results, I expect you have."

"No, not one," said he.

Then I exclaimed, "How is it possible for you to attain these results?"

"Just this way," he replied. "All my men are hand-picked. I accept no
man as a soldier until I talk with him personally. When a raw recruit comes
before me I ask, 'Do you smoke?"

"Yes," he replies; "all Chinese do."

"Do you drink?" "Yes; most Chinese do."

"Do you gamble?" "Yes, for on occasion most Chinese do."

"Then," continued the marshal, "I would say to him: I am your leader, yet I cannot afford to waste money like that, nor precious time, either. I expect you would not be a soldier if you were not a poor man. You can't afford this waste. We have an army savings-bank; if you have twenty or thirty cents to spare, just deposit it in the bank, and when it has increased to forty or fifty dollars we will send it home to your parents. They will certainly be delighted and conclude that their son is not living a fast life. You will get credit at home, and so will I. At once the recruit falls in with my plan and I have no more trouble."

To return to Mr. Wang, the Hanlin scholar. In mentioning the first condition he gave me the opening I needed. "You tell me," I said, "that you don't want to have anything to do with Jesus. For fifty-eight years you have used the eyes He gave you. He gave you good eyes, else you could not have attained to the Hanlin degree. Now since you do not want to have anything to do with Jesus you had better pluck your eyes out and cast them away from you." He seemed very much puzzled, and said, "I did not know that He gave me my eyes." Side by side we sat, and I showed him from John 1:2 and Hebrews 1: 2 and 3 that every organ of his body, as well as the clothes he wore, the food he ate, and the earth he walked upon all came from Jesus. The outcome was that within an hour and a half he was a confessed follower of the Lord Jesus Christ. Later on Mr. Wang became more enthusiastic in proclaiming the doctrines of Jesus Christ than in teaching the Confucian classics.

In 1926, through the combination of powerful enemies, Marshal Feng's army was driven back to the northwest. Some time before this happened Marshal Feng and his chiefs were discussing what they should do to deepen religious conviction among the men. Some suggested this plan, and some suggested that, but Marshal Feng said, "Our great need is spiritual revival, and, referring back to my past work along that line in the army, the Marshal suggested I should be sent for. As a result I received in Canada a letter from General Chang Chih-Chiang and a cable from General Lu Chung-Lin. On receiving these invitations in the early part of 1926, we immediately started back to China. Owing to the fighting, we were unable to get through the lines to Marshal Feng's army. In the meantime he took the trip to Russia. We believe that at the time he had a conviction that it was the only way to save his army from destruction. Personally, we believe the visit to Russia was not for his good, nor for the good of China, but when we consider the fact that he and his army were driven into the northwest, where he had no other outlet than Russia, we should be lenient in our judgment.

On Marshal Feng's return from Russia we visited him at Pao-fou in November, 1926. Our conviction was that he had lost his first love. If we decide a man is not a Christian because he loses his first love, then few Christians will be left in our Christian lands.

He assured me that in Moscow he saw "the highest type of Christianity in operation. Though spoken of as "infidels," the Soviet leaders pointed out to him more than three hundred Christian churches in Moscow alone.' As he was telling me this I looked skeptical, and Marshal Feng insisted, "If you don't believe me, go and see for yourself." I then endeavoured, as gently as I could, to explain that the Soviet leaders had deliberately deceived him.

The Soviet had done its utmost to fill Marshal Feng's mind with hatred against foreign nations, and especially against Britain. For a time we were in sharp disagreement. Marshal Feng is a true patriot. He loves his country. He keenly feels China's humiliation and shame. China is not mistress within her own borders, and never can be considered so as long as foreign concessions remain. It is to be expected that the more genuine the patriot, the more deeply will he feel this wrong. Both sides blundered into this unnatural situation. It is a hopeful sign that the powers show themselves so willing to find ways and means to do away with "extraterritoriality," which causes the Chinese to feel such a sense of injustice.

I warned Marshal Feng that his attitude was likely to provoke foreign war, in which case I pointed out that China only stood to lose. The provoking of a foreign war could not right the wrong. I assured him that I believed Great Britain and also America desired to put China on an equality with themselves, and that they were willing to change anything in the treaties which was unjust. I told the marshal that personally, with my whole heart, I desired to see China's sovereignty restored, that it was an unnatural thing for foreign police and foreign soldiers to be controlling any part of China. I expressed my conviction that as soon as China could guarantee adequate protection to the lives and property of foreign nationals within her borders, the foreign nations would immediately withdraw all restrictions upon China. We parted as good friends as ever.

On returning to Peking I learned that Great Britain two years before had tried to get a concert of the powers with a view to changing everything in the treaties which was objectionable to China and placing China on an equality with themselves. In this effort Great Britain failed, and during those two years endured the ridicule of the Soviet and the enmity of the Chinese. Then Great Britain came out into the open, revealing her readiness two years before to meet the demands of China. At once I sent the full report to Marshal Feng. He replied expressing his delight to learn that Britain was prepared to treat China so fairly.

Many things adverse to Marshal Feng's reputation as a Christian have been said of him. He has been charged with treachery to his friend, Wu Pei-fu. I reply to that: "Under the same conditions, I, too, would be a traitor to my friend. A man's country is always a bigger thing than his friend. If I am convinced that my friend is taking a certain course which I believe to be harmful to my country, and I have done my utmost to dissuade him from that course, and if, in spite of all I can do, he still persists, I must turn against my friend and stand for country. That is all that Marshal Feng and his officers did to justify the charge of 'treachery.'"

It once appeared in the American papers that the "so-called Christian general" had destroyed most of the peopled dwellings between Weihwei and Changte, a distance of sixty miles, and that he had massacred eighty thousand people. This was simply to hold him up to execration. As soon as possible I got information from one of the most reliable Chinese pastors living in that district. His report was to the effect that a rebellious secret society, called "the Red Spears," by a surprise attack in force had overcome Marshal Feng's garrison stationed at Changte, and had massacred all of them. Marshal Feng then sent General Lu Chung-Lin to restore the situation. He defeated "the Red Spears" captured eight hundred of them, and had them all shot, but did not destroy their homes. This was in accordance with the rules of war, but eight hundred had increased to eighty thousand when the news had crossed the Pacific Ocean.

Most of the things said against Marshal Feng to try and make mock of him as a Christian have no more substantial foundation. We heard the report that Marshal Feng had beaten his first wife to death. We had known them for many years and knew the harmony which existed between them, therefore could give no credence to this story. Later on my wife asked one of the nurses in the Rockefeller Hospital in Peking in regard to this report. She said, "Why, no! Mrs. Feng died of typhoid fever in this hospital, and Marshal Feng visited her daily."

Later on, when Marshal Feng married again, the Rev. Marcus Ch'eng said that he took train from Hankow with the purpose of going to Kalgan to visit the marshalls army. On the way up to Peking, fellow-travelers told him that Marshal Feng was in great trouble. They said that his second wife had run away and left him, carrying away six million dollars with her. On arrival at Peking Mr. Ch'eng inquired about it, and was informed that the thing was only too true and that now Marshal Feng was proceeding with a divorce suit against his wife. Mr. Ch'eng went on up to Kalgan and was met at the station by Marshal Feng. They walked over to his home, and Mr. Ch'eng sat down to dinner with Mrs. Feng, the marshal, and the children. He said that he had never realized a more Christian atmosphere than was evident at that meal.

Once I was a guest in a large company at Peitaiho, where an American lady spoke right out, saying, "Marshal Feng has three young concubines"

"Nonsense!" I retorted. "He has one wife, but no concubine." This woman reiterated her assertion, declaring that her daughter and son-in-law living right beside Marshal Feng's home in Kalgan had seen these three young concubines romping around in the marshals garden.

"I assure you he has no concubines," I continued. "His eldest daughter, Fu Neng, is a large girl about sixteen years of age. Her sister, Fu Fa, is about fifteen, also a large-bodied girl. They have a cousin who has lived with them for years who must be eighteen or nineteen years of age. Then, because your daughter and her husband saw these three young girls romping around in Marshal Feng's garden, they send out this wrong report." If

I had not at that moment checked the slander, it might soon have gone the round of the American papers.

Marshal Feng has been branded as "a communist." At one time the influence of Russia on him was undoubtedly strong, but that is equally true of Chiang Kai-Shek, the President of China. Both these leaders had their eyes opened to the Russian menace at about the same time. Since then they have done their utmost to stamp out Communism in China.

The following is from the pen of Marcus Ch'eng, formerly chaplain-general of Marshal Feng's army: "Feng is an enigma. This is what multitudes are saying in China and elsewhere. So much is said and written, for and against him, but we who know him intimately regard him as the most misunderstood of men, alike by enemies and friends. What a storm of criticism, misrepresentation, opinions, and speculation the poor man has been undergoing and still is going through! It is a wonder that he still lives. It reminds one of the story of a proofreader who, in reading the proofs of a novel, discovered that the printer had made the heroine, who was to die of an overdose of opium, die of an overdose of opinion."

During April of 1929 I visited Marshal Feng in Shensi Province, and spent three days with him. Almost immediately, after exchanging greetings, he in the most humble and Christian fashion begged my pardon for the way he had spoken to me at Pao t'ou in 1926. He said to me:

"Don't come to the conclusion that I am not a Christian because you do not see Christianity in operation in my army as you used to. Remember, when you were with us at Peking our own army was only thirty thousand strong. At that time we were all of one accord and one mind. The whole spirit of the army was that of a Christian body. About half of them were already baptized. Now my army has expanded to several hundred thousand. With me there are two noted Mohammedan generals. There is also a noted Buddhist general. Since China now stands for freedom in religion, it would ill become me to force my opinions upon others. All that I can do now is by my example to show my army and the world what a Christian ought to be."

What more could be expected of a man in his position? Yet some call him an apostate from the faith.

During my visit in April, 1929, I met several times a day with men who were out-and-out Christians. One had the rank of general; the other was the governor of a province. In talking about the slanders against Marshal Feng which had gone the world over, they insisted: "If he is not a Christian, what is he? We who are in daily contact with him cannot but feel that all his words and all his deeds are those of a Christian. Who has ever heard of him having two wives at the same time? All other generals of note have a number of wives. Moreover, if there be an important post to fill, our observation is that Marshal Feng will find a Christian to fill it if possible. For example, take his college at Kaifengfu. There are over two thousand men in that college, training to become magistrates in the six provinces which Marshal Feng now controls. You know the president of that college. He is one of the finest Christians in the land." When I was in Kaifengfu a few days earlier, the president of that college, as soon as he heard that I had arrived, hurried over to see me. Our whole conversation was that of two Christians. Putting my hand on his shoulder and looking into his face, I asked, "How is it between you and your Lord?

With that charming smile of his he said, "It is just the same as you have always known it to be."

During the three days I spent with the marshal in 1929 I felt more drawn to him than I had ever been. Before visiting him I had heard that he was ill, and I found that he was evidently suffering from heart trouble and dropsy. That was not to be wondered at, because for years he had been carrying several men's burdens. I advised him to get change and rest as soon as possible. "I know I need it," he replied, "but how is it possible in China for me to get it?" Then he asked if I would arrange along with my wife to accompany him and his family over to Canada and there arrange for a year's rest and treatment. If he had turned away from Christianity, would he have asked a missionary to associate with him and arrange this trip for him? A few weeks later the arrangements had gone so far that even the passages were spoken for; but the project failed to carry through because at the time the Nanking government would not grant him a diplomatic passport.

For years the *Peking & Tientsin Times* under the editorship of Mr. Wood head seemed to go out of its way to disparage Marshal Feng. But now for the last three years this paper has been his strongest defender.

During the past four years Marshal Feng and his men have seen a good deal of fighting. They have met with both success and adversity, but Feng Yu-Hsiang has shown himself to be a man as great in defeat as in victory.

The results obtained by Marshal Feng in the provinces over which he had temporary control prove him to be equally great as a civil administrator and a military leader. Today he is a poor man because he never tried to enrich himself at the expense of the people. When he had control of Honan Province for six months he instituted a financial policy which, as far as I know, had never been seen in China before. All income and all expenditures were tabulated in the open, on the walls of his yatnen, for public inspection.

I have had opportunity to know Marshal Feng as perhaps no other foreigner. I still believe him to be a Christian. Though he seems in a measure to have backslidden, yet I believe the Lord has given unto him eternal life and shall not let him perish, but will bring him to new obedience. His case is a challenge to Christians to keep on persevering in prayer for him. I never let a day pass without praying for him.

THE END.

SCRIPTURE TESTIMONY INDEX

Disciples must keep their word 2
Matthew 5:37

Dr. McClure and Dr. Goforth, both committed Christians, demonstrated unwavering integrity as they honored their word to the blind chief of police. Despite initial skepticism, they returned six months later as promised, restoring the chief's sight through a successful operation, affirming their commitment to honesty and compassion.

God leads believers in opposition to idolatry 3
Acts 17:16-17 · 1 Corinthians 8:4 · 1 John 5:21

The Goforths and Chou Lao-chang, a local convert, were led by the Lord to stand firmly against a popular male-child-giving goddess in North Honan. With firmness and conviction, they proclaimed God's power over and above any man-made God and were blessed to win some souls over from idolatry to Christianity.

God using an inner voice to communicate 6
John 14:26 · Acts 10:19-20 · Acts 11:12

Despite her hesitation, the Spirit of the Lord continued to impress an instruction upon Rosalind Goforth's heart and when she finally yielded, a great harvest of souls was witnessed!

Salvation transforms 9
2 Corinthians 5:16-17 · Galatians 6:15

Dr. Goforth and Mr. MacGillivray hired Mr. Wang Feng-ao as their Chinese instructor, despite warnings of his bad temper. Through their religious studies, Mr. Wang had a change of heart, embraced Christianity, and his wife, who was already a secret believer, found comfort in openly professing her faith.

Jesus is able to save to the uttermost.. 14
Hebrews 7:25

In China, a skilled storyteller named Wang Fu-lin fell into opium addiction which destroyed his career. With the help of Dr. Malcolm, Wang Fu-lin overcame his addiction after a harrowing experience, leading to his transformation from a wreck to a trustworthy man who eventually contributed to the Gospel work despite facing extreme hardships.

God's work will not lack God's supply.................................... 17
Philippians 4:19

In 1895, in Changte, the Goforths faced immense curiosity from the locals as they shared the Gospel despite having no support. When they prayed for help, Wang Fu-lin, a seemingly humble beggar in appearance, arrived and proved to be an exceptional preacher, convincing even the educated class with his logical and persuasive storytelling.

By faith, those who believe in Jesus are truly saved.................... 21
John 10:1-14 · Acts 13:38-39 · Romans 10:13 · Colossians 2:13-14 · 1 John 4:17

Wang-Mei, a devout follower of the Sheng Taot sect, embarked on arduous pilgrimages to earn merit. Despite his efforts, he only found true peace and purpose after encountering Christianity through his friend Ho-I, and eventually embraced salvation by grace alone, experiencing great joy and inner peace.

Beaten for preaching the Gospel... 36
Acts 5:40 · Acts 14:19-20

During 1900, the year of the Boxer Rebellion, Mr. Ho and his companions faced danger in Changte city due to their Christian preaching. When faced with the decision to flee to safety or stay and face the consequences, Mr. Ho and the Chinese believers chose to stand with the missionaries, risking their lives for their faith in Jesus Christ. Despite facing ridicule, disgrace, and threats of violence, Mr. Ho bravely proclaimed his newfound faith to the authorities, emphasizing his transformation from an idol-maker and lawbreaker to a follower of the Living and True God.

Holy Spirit convicts people of their sin 43
John 16:8

In Ta Kwan-Chwang, God's revival was hindered until Wang-I, the chief man in the church, confessed to his sins and made amends for his dishonesty, ultimately leading to a resurgence of faith in the community. His confession and repentance not only led to the construction of a new church, but also inspired many to seek salvation, leaving a lasting impact on those around him until his peaceful passing.

Believers will suffer terrible things for the sake of Jesus' name 57
Matthew 24:9-14

Dr. Goforth noticed Chang-san's keen interest in Christianity during a street chapel preaching session. Despite his father's violence and the village's disapproval, Chang-san bravely declared his faith in Jesus, leading to a dangerous confrontation with his father, "The Fury," who attempted to harm him for converting to Christianity.

As we serve Him, the Lord will be our defense 66
Luke 10:19 · 2 Thessalonians 3:1-3

Rosalind Goforth recounts a day of village preaching with her Bible women, including the risky decision to bring Mary along despite the threat of infectious disease. Even though smallpox was present in the village, Mary was miraculously kept safe, and her presence helped in bridging the gap with the heathen women in a profound way.

There is no sting in death for the believer 68
1 Corinthians 15:54-57

When a sick young girl and her mother found the Lord Jesus, they so embraced him that the young girl became fearless even in the face of death for she knew that for every believer in Christ Jesus, death has lost its sting.

Don't put off the decision for salvation............................... 69
Acts 24:25 · 2 Corinthians 6:2 · James 4:14

Chang, a bread maker in Hsiwen, was a severe gambler who squandered his family's fortune. His daughter's illness led to a change in their family, with her and her mother embracing Christianity, while Chang continued to gamble recklessly. Despite warnings, Chang met a sudden demise in a gambling den, highlighting the consequences of his actions and serving as a cautionary tale against delaying the decision to accept God's gift of salvation.

Believers exchange superstition for faith in Christ..................... 73
Acts 19:18-19

Captain Li-Ming, a powerful militia commander with three wives, became deeply interested in the Gospel after initially hearing about it in Changte city and later purchasing a Christian catechism. His decisive act of burning his household gods led to his entire household embracing Christianity, and they found newfound peace and love for each other as a result of their shared faith.

Deliverance from enemies and circumstances........................... 75
Luke 1:71

Captain Li, a man of strong faith, demonstrated the power of prayer as he trusted in God to protect his crops from locusts while his neighbors' fields were destroyed. Li-ming used this miraculous event to share the story of God's intervention in his life as he preached in various villages, proving the truth of his words through the testimony of those who witnessed the extraordinary event.

Protest against those unwilling to hear the Gospel..................... 82
Matthew 10:14 · Mark 6:11 · Luke 9:5

Despite facing hostility and disturbances while preaching in villages with Shantung preachers, a turning point came when Dr Goforth referenced Matthew 10: 14,15, leading to the villagers ceasing their opposition and even requesting more preaching sessions in the future.

Jesus is able to save to the uttermost.. 88
Hebrews 7:25

Kwoa was once a destitute man consumed by addiction to opium, but with the help of his Christian friends from Changtsun, he was brought to a meeting to be saved. Through prayer, support, and perseverance, Kwoa overcame his cravings and was transformed into an eloquent preacher, testifying to the transformative power of Jesus in his life, where he regained his property, family, and a brighter future.

The heart of the believer, like Jesus, is full of compassion 97
Matthew 9:36-38 · Galatians 6:2 · Ephesians 4:32 · Colossians 3:12

Dr. Goforth had a conversation with a noted scholar who noticed a globe in his study and was led to discussions about astronomy and eventually about the one true God. The scholar pondered over the motives of foreign missionaries in China, especially impressed by their selfless actions like providing medical care and education, leading him to understand the love of Christ and accept the idea of salvation before his passing.

God answers prayer.. 104
Luke 18:7 · John 15:7 · Acts 12:5 · James 5:15

In the Sun-tao region, there were many bandits causing trouble, but through the work of Dr. Goforth, ex-bandit Mr. Tung and others, converts began to multiply. As the need for more workers became apparent, Chang-Ching, two government-school teachers, and a former opium addict, Kwoa Lao-T'swei, in answers to prayer, stepped up to preach the Gospel, joining others sent by the Lord to help spread the word.

Demons cast out in Jesus' name 106
Matthew 8:16-17 · Matthew 8:28-32 · Matthew 9:32-34 · Mark 1:23-26 · Mark 9:20-27 · Luke 10:17

In Sun-tao, a famous witch doctor named Ch'en Lao-Jung struggled to free his mother from a powerful demon, but failed. When he sought help, a Christian prayed to God and the old woman was free, bringing peace and joy to the family's home.

Jesus is able to save to the uttermost...................................... 115
Hebrews 7:25

Mr. Su, a man who was initially drawn to vices like drinking, gambling, and women, experienced a life-changing encounter at a Christian meeting where he heard a message that convicted him of his sins. This led to a radical transformation in his life, causing him to abandon his old ways and become a dedicated follower of Christ, even in the face of opposition from his family and society.

God using circumstances and timing to communicate............... 129
Acts 11:11

Cornelia Bonnell, while at Vassar, faced physical and financial challenges as she prepared to follow her calling to China. Despite initial obstacles and doubts, she eventually found her way to Shanghai with the support of Martha Jewell, eager to fulfill her mission of helping the women in the red-light district, which was confirmed as God's will through a series of events.

God's work will not lack God's supply..................................... 134
Philippians 4:19

During a time of turmoil in Shanghai, the Door of Hope struggled to find a safe place to rent until Miss Abercrombie organized a prayer meeting with the workers and girls. Despite initial resistance, a wealthy Chinese man eventually changed his mind and allowed them to rent a more suitable place, showing that sometimes our loving father answers prayer even before we finish.

God answers prayer.. 139
Luke 18:7 · John 15:7 · Acts 12:5 · James 5:15

Dr. Mary Stone and Miss Hughes' evangelistic efforts and the operation of a mission in Shanghai was financially blessed from unexpected sources, such as receiving a last-minute check in the post office to pay contractors and a chance encounter leading to a telephone connection. Despite financial challenges, their faith and prayer sustained the mission's growth.

Lay down one's life for another 145
John 15:12-13 · Ephesians 5:2 · 1 John 3:16-18

In a touching incident witnessed by General Feng, then an unbeliever, during the Boxer Rebellion, a missionary named Miss Morrell selflessly offered her life to save others, ultimately inspiring some to spare lives before tragically being massacred.

Elijah, a normal human being, prayed for rain............................151
James 5:17

During a severe drought in Honan Province, General Feng gathered his army to pray for rain. Despite some doubts about his conversion, the extraordinary faith of Marshal Feng and his men resulted in rain falling in both Hunan and Honan Provinces after their prayers.

Believers are the aroma of Christ to those around them............. 153
2 Corinthians 2:14-16

Marshal Feng achieved discipline in his army through the power of his personal example; he personally selected soldiers, emphasizing financial responsibility over vices like smoking, drinking, and gambling, leading to success without needing strict rules against such behaviors in the army.

Walking Together Press is a non-profit publishing company devoted to supporting grassroots libraries in Africa through global book sales and through providing free library editions.

To read our story, to see our catalog, and to learn more about how you can help us in our mission, visit our website at:

walkingtogether.press